Totally Awesome

Stephen P. Dietzel

Bloomington, IN  Milton Keynes, UK

authorHOUSE®

AuthorHouse™
1663 Liberty Drive, Suite 200
Bloomington, IN 47403
www.authorhouse.com
Phone: 1-800-839-8640

AuthorHouse™ UK Ltd.
500 Avebury Boulevard
Central Milton Keynes, MK9 2BE
www.authorhouse.co.uk
Phone: 08001974150

First published by AuthorHouse 4/26/2007

ISBN: 978-1-4343-0124-6 (sc)

Printed in the United States of America
Bloomington, Indiana

This book is printed on acid-free paper.

Dedication

Totally Awesome is dedicated to my personal angel and sweetheart, Judy, and our super son, Paul, who each add zest to a life over blessed. It is written with the prayer that God may receive all the glory. My fondest hope is that you may catch a glimpse of the Hidden Treasure that is available to all. May God bless you beyond your belief as you begin to Think on these things!

Stephen P. Dietzel

PREFACE

From revivals, banquets and church retreats, to seminars on self-image and motivational leadership, the desire of my heart has been to challenge people to move from the realm of the spectator to the participant in the abundant Christian life. It is so easy to sit contentedly in the arena of life and watch with the cheering crowds.

God calls us to be competitors not merely onlookers. Our fellowship with Him strengthens relationships with husband and wife, family, business associates, acquaintances and even those people who may cross our paths only once. The game of life goes on...so too must we.

Totally Awesome has been on my mind and in my thoughts for years. Since the time I was old enough to remember, my Dad has had that special secret ingredient around which this book revolves. There is one missing link that causes heroes to stand above the crowd. He taught me by the way he lived to treat everyone as a unique and gifted person.

From the LSU trainer, Herman Lang, to the South Carolina grounds keeper, Sarge Frye - everyone was special. From the All-American athlete to the young man in the iron lung, Dad had a natural yet uncanny love for people.

The blessings of this book are Totally Awesome for me. It is one of my greatest thrills to pick-up these powerful truths from my bedside stand, the kitchen table or the rack by my living-room chair. This book is to be read and reread as a reminder. It is a reminder of that divine and miraculous Totally Awesome experience the Lord provides all those who trust in Him. It is a refresher to enlighten our thoughts and minds with some of God's greatest gifts.

Contents

HIDDEN TREASURE!

You are about to discover the hidden treasure...the unsolved mystery...the missing ingredient. It may be more dramatic than the latest big screen motion picture. It might be more valuable to you than any other secret you've ever known. It could be the lone key to unlock riches in every area of your life. It is one of the simplest, yet most complex of all truth.

My favorite story as a child was about the little boy who had to walk home after football practice each day by a big, scary and gruesome graveyard. Day after day he would take the traditional walk around that dark and foreboding place, just as the sun disappeared behind the horizon.

One lone night, after many journeys around the graveyard, he courageously cut through that lifeless field of tombstones. He tripped along whistling and confident until he really did trip into an open grave. Picture yourself in that dark deep hole for a moment!

He jumped and he jumped trying to get out of the dark graveyard tomb. Finally, realizing there was no way out, the little boy curled up in the cold corner. He would have to endure the dark and lonely night and wait until morning.

About that time, one of his buddies came bopping down the same dark path. You guessed it! Into the same grave he fell, literally head over heals! The little boy in the corner remained quiet, waiting for the opportune time to *encourage* his friend.

After his buddy jumped up and down for what seemed like hours, the first little boy seized his opportunity. He quietly slipped over and tapped his buddy on the back, whispering, "You're not gettin' out!" **WHOOOOOM!** That little boy catapulted out of the six feet deep hole, clearing it by three feet! He was motivated for action!

Here's the question...did he discover some unique hidden treasure, some inner magic motivator, some missing ingredient necessary to propel him to higher heights? Was he merely motivated for the moment? Circumstances such as exciting events and activities can often motivate you and me to provide stellar temporary performances. That is all they are however, temporary.

Life is a long-distance marathon not just a sprint. The tapes and books we buy to motivate us to maximum potential often fail to promote or encourage long-term change. Our purpose here is beyond the temporary. You will discover the missing ingredient that will motivate you permanently!

We are goal-oriented people. We need challenges in life to help motivate us to maximize our talents and abilities. Challenges add a real *zest* and *pizzaz* to life. We need to set goals that are Achievable, Believable, Conceivable, Desirable - A...B...C...D...and E. Could "**E**" be the missing ingredient, the secret hidden treasure?

Let's look at a second little boy who was excited, but for a different reason. It was the night before Christmas, and all through the house, the crackling of paper - could it be a mouse? No, it was our little friend carefully unwrapping a long-awaited gift from Santa. The special shiny red wagon glistened in the moonlight before it was rewrapped for Christmas morn!

The next day the little minister's son awoke bright and early. Into the living room he raced to the lights and bright colors of the tinseled tree that shadowed his special gift. He ripped open the package - now for a second time. WOW! He exclaimed with glee - it's my red wagon! What a surprise - ha!

He hurriedly began putting the wheels on the wagon, pushing directions aside. The first wheel stubbornly went on, then suddenly fell off. The wagon tipped over. G-O-L-L-L-E-Y! exclaimed the little boy.

"Son, we don't use that kind of language," said the preacher Daddy. Just say, "Praise the Lord!" The little boy smiled and jammed the first wheel on again. Then came the second wheel. Much as the first, it was on, then off both wheels fell........... G-O-L-L-L-E-Y!

Now somewhat perturbed, yet calmly and patiently the minister Dad again said, "Son, please don't use that language. Just say, Praise the Lord in all circumstances." The little boy smiled, and carefully began placing the first wheel, then the second, and the third in their appropriate places. He turned his proud head around with a smile, and he put the fourth wheel in place. All of a sudden all four wheels fell off the wagon.

"PRAISE THE LORD!" shouted the little boy. WHAAAAP! The four wheels miraculously popped back onto the wagon...and the preacher Daddy roared, "G-O-L-L-L-E-Y!!!!"

We need to move from G-O-I-L-L-E-Y to PRAISE THE LORD. We are often so content with the golly, and so startled by the miraculous that we never expect it. We must master the missing ingredient. We must find the hidden treasure before it is too late.

The missing ingredient is not gained from a motivational speaker or book, or through the experience of a tremendous athletic event or fine arts performance. It is not realized because we have "been in the right place at the right time," like the little boys. Typically, there is only one challenge that will motivate you permanently.

One of the greatest retailers, F.W. Woolworth said, "A man can succeed in anything if for that thing he has it." Ralph Waldo Emerson, renowned author, declared, "No great act has ever been accomplished without it." Perhaps the world's greatest historian, Arnold Toynbee discovered, "It is the only thing that can overcome apathy."

IT became apparent to me as a young boy in the late nineteen-fifties. Growing up the son of a well-known football coach has a lot of glitter for a child. The advantages were so awesome that if there were disadvantages they were never recognized. Above the roar of the crowd one message was indelibly inscribed on my mind, at the age of nine years old. The title of the message was "CHAMP." What is a "CHAMPION?" Dad would say, as he spoke to thousands of athletes at hundreds of banquets and assemblies throughout the country.

"**CHAMP**." The "**C**" stands for challenge. Everyone in life, every athlete, every scholar, every artist in whatever field of endeavor was once inspired by a personal challenge. God created us to be goal-oriented and goal-motivated individuals. For some, a challenge drives a person to heights only enjoyed by the fantastic few. For the "superstars" in life a challenge motivates miraculous movement day-after-day.

The "**H**" in Champ stands for help. No man is an island. No individual can really succeed in life without the help of others. Every success story you have ever heard about a champion has involved many people who were there to "help" that person attain a level in life rarely accomplished as a loner. We must have help from others to be champions in life. No individual can run the race, or play the game of life alone! No Olympic champion ever gained the gold alone. He or she was inspired, encouraged, trained and lead by at least one who helped.

The "**A**" represents "adhere" to the rules. The high school football player ran into the stands and galloped the full length of the field, strutting back onto the turf at the goal line. The whistle blew, the fans roared - in disapproval and disbelief. The run was magnificent - but it didn't count. The boy was out-of-bounds - he failed to follow the rules.

The little first grader named Michael was the joy of the basketball team as he drove for the first basket. He dribbled recklessly and fearlessly to lead the team. He had every good intention, but shot at the wrong end of the court. The whistle blew. The basket did not count. He didn't mean to do so, but he failed to follow the rules. Successful people are motivated and even challenged by the "rules" in the game of life. We must adhere to the rules!

The "**M**" of Champ stands for maximum effort. Lt. Colonel Clebe McClary leaped-out of the foxhole to throw his fearless but fragile body across the explosion of a hand-grenade. He saved the lives of his soldier buddies, but sacrificed an arm and an eye of his own. As a college athlete in South Carolina it was my personal privilege to know Clebe and his precious bride Deanna. Often I heard Clebe say, "In this world of give and take, few are willing to give what it takes." It takes maximum effort for a person to become successful, to be a champion in his or her chosen field. A half-hearted, lackadaisical attempt at anything produces only a "lukewarm" result. Maximum effort causes the champion to give beyond himself, beyond his capacity - to give whatever it takes!

The "**P**" of Champ represents a tried, trusted and true statement we have all heard. A Champion "pays the price" to be victorious. A Champion pays the price to be a leader in the game of life. The price was paid by another who was a boyhood hero of mine, growing up in the bayou land of south Louisiana.

He was a former LSU All-American, runner-up to the heralded Heisman Trophy, All-Pro many years with the St. Louis Cardinals and former head football coach of the LSU Fighting Tigers. Jerry Stovall walked the talk as he said, "Victory is expensive, but CHAMPIONS

5

PAY THE PRICE!"

YOU too are a champion in life. There's nobody else in the whole human race with your kind of style and your kind of grace. There's nobody else exactly like you, there's nobody else like you! Nobody else is given the capacity to be the best YOU except YOU! You have got the goods! Nobody else can have it for you!

For many years I have thought about and reminisced on the *championship life style* I heard from and saw in my Dad. Life has always been a really exciting challenge for me. The secret, the hidden treasure, the unsolved mystery is no mystery at all. It was there all the time - yet, is seldom discovered. You can discover the hidden treasure of life - but with it you must also take the responsibility to give it away.

Don't race so quickly through the luxuries of life that you miss it. Don't pass by the greatest gift that God has endowed upon His creation. The gift is priceless and precious, yet, so simply wrapped. Many will trip along spending half their lives in open graves without it! Please don't miss it. Capture it!

Pretty obvious by now, isn't it? The "**E**" of our Achievable –Believable – Conceivable - Desirable equation is **ENTHUSIASM!** *Enthusiasm* is much bigger and broader than you have ever imagined. It is not simply the backslapper, or the guy with the sunshine grin or the bone-crushing handshake.

"Enthusiasm" comes from two little Greek words, "an Theos," meaning "in God" or "God within." It is something on the inside. It is a heart attitude. Enthusiasm is an inside job!

Enthusiasm is one common attitude that is characteristic of all successful people. Think about highly motivated and successful people you know. As a youth my heroes were Olympian Bob Richards, New York Yankee second baseman, Bobby Richardson, Dallas Quarterback

Roger Staubach and Coach Tom Landry.

I had the thrill of meeting and knowing each of those giants of the athletic world. Nearly all of us remember Johnny Wooden of UCLA, perhaps the greatest basketball coach who ever lived. Perhaps the greatest football coach was Vince Lombardi of the Green Bay Packers.

Less than six-feet tall, but a giant of enthusiasm in the military was General Douglas MacArthur. Norman Vincent Peale probably wrote as many books on positive attitudes and enthusiasm as any other person who ever lived.

Billy Graham, enthusiastic for the Gospel, has become one of the greatest leaders ever in worldwide evangelism. At his side were Bev Shay and Cliff Barrows, two more pillars of enthusiasm in gospel music. To have the privilege of personally meeting these men gave me a wonderful perspective on the abundant, life of enthusiasm that only God can give.

Each of those men radiate an inner enthusiasm that overwhelms even a brief handshake. Some people just seem to radiate an inner enthusiasm that is divine and beautiful. IT only comes from a supernatural, spectacular, and **AWESOME** Heavenly Father.

Earl Nightingale, Dale Carnegie, Og Mandino, and William Danforth have impacted thousands and thousands of lives as they lived a life of enthusiasm. Zig Zigler, Paul Harvey, Dennis Waitely and Charles Stanley - the list is endless of those who have impacted our entire country. Many have even had a tremendous impact upon the entire world because they had that extra, but often missing ingredient called "enthusiasm!" No other character trait can drive a person towards success in every endeavor in such a way as **ENTHUSIASM**!

Where do you find it? How do you get it? Does it just happen? Do you seek it? Can you learn it, or earn it? This book is dedicated to enabling you to not only discover, but unwrap and fully utilize the gift, the hidden treasure.

Once you have it, there is a totally awesome responsibility that goes along with it. Once you have it, there is no better way to expand or magnify it in your life than to give it away. You only have one chance to make a good first impression.

You only have one life to live, and there are "Little Eyes Upon You" as you journey. Read on with **E N T H U S I A S M** . . .

LITTLE EYES UPON YOU

There are little eyes upon you, and they're watching night and day,
There are little ears that quickly take in every word you say,

There are little hands all eager to do anything you do,
And a little guy who's dreaming of the day he'll be like you.

You're the little fellow's idle, you're the wisest of the wise,
In his little mind about you no suspicions ever rise.

He believes in you devoutly holds that all you say and do,
He will say and do your way, when he grows up like you.

There's a wide-eyed little fellow who believes you're always right,
And his ears are always open and he watches day and night.

You are setting an example every day in all you do,
For the little guy who's waiting to grow up to be like you.

Author Unknown

The World is Yours!

You will read many motivational and encouraging thoughts in this book. Very few of them are original. My favorite was on a little wood plaque in a store-front, "If it is the **TRUTH**, does it matter who said it?" I have read and studied, and tried to live "the truth" for so long I can't remember if I said it, or read it!

The "**TRUTH**" again is this, "**ENTHUSIASM**" is an inside job. It has to come from within your heart. I didn't think that up either. Remember "an Theos" - in God, God within - it's a heart attitude. It's an inside deal! And, there's more good news: Once you have it, you can't lose it, as you'll see!

"We become what we think about." "What the mind of man can believe and conceive, the mind of man can achieve." Man didn't think that up! Meditate upon Proverbs 23:7: *"As a man thinks in his heart, so is he* [or she].*"*

If you have ever studied sales you are aware of the fact that only 15-20% of the success enjoyed by all professional salespeople is due to product knowledge and actual job skills. Real sales' success is produced in the area of attitudes. Nothing is more important than an enthusiastic attitude.

When you are enthusiastic about something, other people get caught up in it. People want to be around someone who has an infectious, enthusiastic attitude in life. It is usually easier to "buy" the products, services or even ideas of an enthusiastic person. Inner conviction and belief characterize enthusiastic and believable expression.

Why be enthusiastic? It is always more fulfilling to live a life of enthusiasm. A smile is much easier on the face muscles than a frown! It's often more exciting to live on the mountaintop, on the sunny positive side of life, than in the dark dreary valley. We sometimes learn the greatest lessons of life in the valley, but that isn't where we want to live.

Life is too short to be negative and downcast. Make your first impression the best one, because it may be the only one! Too many people are dependent upon you. God has created you to have an impact upon the lives of certain other people that no one else can touch. Live your life to its fullest by being a "lifter," an encourager to those around you. Enthusiasm dramatically affects you, and allows you to affect others.

Let me illustrate one of the values of enthusiasm. If I were to give you a million dollars tonight, what would you do with it? New car, house, clothes? You wouldn't have time to buy any of those things today, but, TODAY, your attitude would change! You would definitely have at least a momentary excitement about your life today. Put your mind into a temporary state of belief - believe you really do have the million dollars right now!

Dream for a minute... Some of you real innovative thinkers are already thinking how nice that would be, and what you would do with your money. You would pay off the house, the cars, and all the credit cards. You would set aside about one-hundred thousand dollars for each child's education - that's what it will cost in the years numbered 2000+! You would buy your spouse a new wardrobe, and plan a vacation or two!

Pause for a few minutes and write down your "million dollar" list. Imagine everything you could buy or do with that one million dollars. Really dream - let your mind go. Write down your wildest wishes. Do it now - write it down. As you pay off the smaller accounts apply that monthly payment to the next prioritized debt:

1. Date to Pay-off major accounts: _____

2. Date to Pay-off the cars: _____

3. Date to Pay off the house: _____

4. Date to Add to retirement: _____

5. Date to Add to education fund: _____

6. Date to Plan vacation(s): _____

7. Date to Plan _____: _____

Enjoy the luxury of thinking as a member of "The Rich and Famous" rather than "The Proud and Poor!" With one-million dollars would your lifestyle change any? You bet it would! You would probably enjoy financial freedom, being out of debt and not having to worry about the month that's left every four weeks after the money! Of course for most people, the more you make the more you spend - but be different!

Start paying off debts and providing for the future. Begin by spending less than you make (that's been a tough lesson for us to learn). At this moment in time all you are doing is dreaming - but if you can't visualize and imagine goals and ideals you have for yourself you will never realize them. Perhaps money is not important to you.

There is nothing wrong with having it, or not having it. The Bible tells us "the love of money is the root of all evil," not the possession of it.

The point is this, if we "seek first His Kingdom and His righteousness, all these things will be added. Financial freedom is still the American dream, but for ninety-five percent of the people it is only a dream. Those statistics are also pretty accurate for those who achieve success physically, mentally and in relationships with God and people. If you and I do not do something about that fact in the future, the statistics will not change. If we keep doing what we've been doing, we'll keep having what we have - in every realm of life.

Most people cannot even enjoy the dream of attaining anything special in life. Everything is a "scam," or a "get rich quick," or, "it will never happen to me deal." Those people are exactly right - it will never happen! Remember, you become what you think about - so think trash and poverty and that's where you'll live. Zig Zigler calls it "stinkin thinkin." Get rid of it before it destroys you.

Begin a positive plan to achieve the financial goals you have set for yourself, as if you had the one million dollars. You and I may never have that financial luxury, but why not have that million-dollar attitude! Enjoy what you do have. Work on your million-dollar list, and begin to follow your plan. You have to do it one step at a time, or as Charlie Brown once said, "Life is like an ice cream cone, you have to lick it one day at a time." Begin to do it now!

Think how you feel when your attitude is negative. Certainly, you are not excited and on top of the world. Not only do you need to get rid of the negative thinking, you need to begin to believe you have a right to the "good life." Focus upon all the positive blessings you have right now. Replace the negative with positive thoughts!

Dr. H. Edwin Young (Second Baptist Church, Houston, Texas) has always said, "God doesn't sponsor any flops!" The point is **YOU** and **I** were created for a better life than the one for which we have settled! Guaranteed!

We have no idea what abundant life is all about. Believe, just for a minute that **ENTHUSIASM** really does make the difference! Believe for a moment that with enthusiasm you really can accomplish anything you want to accomplish. Believe the Creator of the universe is a wise and discerning God that knows you better than you know yourself. Believe you can become a better YOU, now!

One of the greatest achievements I've ever witnessed in athletics is one of which few people are aware. The year was 1958 at Louisiana State University. The LSU Fighting Tiger football team was composed of three squads: the White Team, the Go Team (short for gold), and the Chinese Bandits. The "third" team was named after Coach Paul Dietzel discovered through a Sunday comic strip that "Chinese Bandits" were the meanest and most vicious people in the world!

The best football players were chosen to play on the White Team. The White Team played both offensively and defensively. The next best athletes became members of the Go Team, which played offense seventy-five percent of the time. The third team, although no one called them that, became The Chinese Bandits. The Bandits were very near and dear to the coach's heart. They would play defense about seventy-five percent of the time, and the coach insured them they would "definitely have a big part in every game."

Coach Dietzel convinced the Chinese Bandits that they were better than they were, so they were! As Coach recalls 1958, "It was the fifth game against Kentucky that was the making of the Chinese Bandits. Had I planned the whole affair, or if I had had a publicity agent in Hollywood fashion prepare the script, it could not have been more spectacular."

Stephen P. Dietzel

At the Coach's direction midway through the first quarter the announcer proclaimed to 68,000 fans -- "Here come the Chinese Bandits!" On the very first play from scrimmage the Kentucky fullback was met in mid air and the ball was knocked out of his hands. The announcer then proclaimed to the cheering throng, "And here come the Chinese Bandits right back!" The rest is history...

By next game the now famous "The Chinese Bandit Chant" hit the airwaves:

> **Chinese Bandits on their way...**
> **Listen to what Confucius say!**
>
> **Chinese Bandits like to knock...**
> **Gonna' stop a touchdown...**
>
> **CHOP! CHOP!**

The 1958 Chinese Bandits continued to accomplish bigger and better things as the season unfolded. The year ended with a January 1, Sugar Bowl victory, an 11-0 season, a National Championship and Coach of the Year honors for Paul Dietzel. "They played like Champions. They were Champions. They were a great pleasure to watch because of their tremendous enthusiasm. The fans loved them for their hustle and utter abandon. I shall never forget the Chinese Bandits," smiles Paul Dietzel.

From the islands of Hawaii, across California to Texas and Louisiana and east to Florida and the Carolinas those that follow football remember the Chinese Bandits. The memory still lingers in Tiger Stadium nearly fifty years later. The LSU Tiger Marching Band brings a great defensive effort off the football field with gongs, symbols and the unmatched musical splendor of the Chinese Bandit chant!

16

The magnificent story of the Chinese Bandits was that they became better than they were because one man convinced them they were better than they were. They believed in themselves, individually and corporately. They attained a championship level of excellence because they believed they could do it.

You too have the gifts and talents to be whatever you want to be, and do whatever you want to do. You have been blessed beyond measure, yet you have not even scratched the surface of your potential. You must believe it - to enjoy it! Start thinking, dreaming, believing and expecting the best. If you don't, you won't! Want to be greater later - think greater now!

Let's go to a different arena. The University of South Carolina Gamecocks had one team member that stood far taller than all the rest. He was an integral part of the USC football team. He never went to a practice, he never dressed-out for or attended a game, yet he was instrumental to the success of the team. He forever made his mark in Columbia, South Carolina. Come with me for a visit.

"There was a place a lot of people went when they needed help... to the Columbia Hospital to visit the boy in the iron lung. People from all walks of life - ministers, athletes, coaches and businessmen - often visited him. They went to borrow something that they needed and that he had in abundance...courage."

His words will forever ring in my ears, "Steve, I am so blessed to be in this first room in the Columbia Hospital. You see, everyone that comes in the hospital has to pass my room. That gives me the chance to tell them about my precious Lord." What a true **CHAMPION**! His name was Gilbert Davis.

Gilbert had no wealth, or possessions, no worldly goods or fame. He had little reason to "celebrate" life, yet he had the missing ingredient. He radiated a charisma and an enthusiasm that brought a glow into the world around him. That glow was the presence of the living God within his life.

On Friday, September 27, 1968, as the Gamecocks were leaving Columbia to meet the North Carolina Tar Heels, Coach Dietzel was told of Gilbert's death. That Saturday, badly beaten and trailing by 27-3, in the fourth quarter, the Gamecocks staged a miraculous comeback to edge the Tar Heels, 32-27.

"What a day this would have been," said Coach Dietzel, if Gilbert could have shared it with us. If I could have gone to his room tomorrow, what a proud thing it would have been for me. Maybe for once in my life I could have said, "You see, Gilbert, some of it did rub off on us." "A mission station was closed at Columbia Hospital early that Friday morning - a mission station where we all went when our hearts needed help" (Herman Helms, "The State" newspaper).

THE WORLD IS YOURS! It really is! Believe it, the best is yet to come. Believe in yourself. You are God's greatest miracle! Your wildest imaginings haven't captured tomorrow's joy. Act like a child of the King! Life is abundant! Be a shouting believer, not a doubting believer! Shout about life. You are blessed. Whoever you are. You are blessed just to be able to hold this book and to read these words. Let **ENTHUSIASM** grip you - from the inside-out!

Read on . . .

The World is Mine!

Today upon a bus I saw a gal with golden hair,
She smiled at me and had such joy, I wished I were as fair.
Then suddenly as she rose to leave, I saw her hobble down the aisle;
She had one foot and wore a crutch, But as she passed, a smile.
Oh God, forgive me when I whine, I have two legs, the world is mine!

Then I stopped to buy some candy, the lad who sold it had such charm.
I talked with him, he seemed so glad, if I were late, it'd do no harm.
And as I left, he said to me, "I thank you, you've been so kind.
It's nice to talk with folks like you. You see," said he, "I'm blind."
Oh God, forgive me when I whine, I have two eyes, the world is mine!

Then walking down the street I saw a child with eyes of blue.
She stood & watched the others play, it seemed she knew not what to do.
I stopped a moment, then I said, "Why don't you join the others, dear?"
She looked ahead without a word, Then I knew, she could not hear.
Oh God, forgive me when I whine, I have two ears, the world is mine!

With feet to take me where I would go, with eyes to see the sunset glow,
With ears to hear what I should know; Oh God, forgive me when I whine,
I'm blessed indeed, the world is mine!

Author Unknown

Awesome Entrance!

Have you ever been to a place that was so magnificent that you wanted to stay indefinitely? Hawaii was such a place for me - the peace, the serenity, the warm yet gentle breeze through the swaying palm trees - the surf sweeping briskly across the sands - the calm and relaxed attitudes of the people.

On our honeymoon Judy and I stayed in the Hyatt Regency on the Island of Maui. What a thrill it was. The only greater thrill - was after we left "paradise" island. There's really no place like home!

Go back to the word *enthusiasm*...God on the inside of your life. If the living God were going to take up dwelling in your life, would it be the kind of place He would be comfortable staying, or would it only be good for a brief visit? Nothing is more special to my sweet wife Judy and me than spending time with our family...and HIS family. Is that true with Christ and you?

Initially, Christ may find some things in each of our lives that are not really pleasing to Him. If we let God be God however, He can take care of the rough edges in our life, if we let Him.

As a young athlete at a conference of the Fellowship of Christian Athletes (FCA), I heard a story that totally changed my life. James

Jeffrey, Executive Director of FCA had four-hundred young athletes spell-bound as he juggled and showed magic tricks in the Estes Park, Colorado chapel. "Jeff" was blessed with that infectious gift, that missing ingredient, and he was totally awesome because of it. The room radiated with the glow of his life as he spoke of "the king."

Back many years ago there lived a wise king who sought a leader for his armies. It so happened he was able to capture a powerful warrior who was reputed to be the greatest that ever lived. The warrior was brought before the king in the magnificent throne room. This mighty and muscular man stood before the throne. At his side were his faithful wife and his proud son. The king told the warrior he would be asked three questions. Based upon the answers given to the questions the king would decide the fate of the soldier.

"The first question is this," said the king. "What would you do for me if I were to spare your life? The warrior calmly responded, "I would never fight against you again." The king quietly accepted the answer.

The second question posed by the king was this, "What would you do for me faithful warrior if I were to spare the life of your young son?" The warrior proudly looked at his boy and turned to the king saying, "I would lead your armies into battle and protect your throne to make you the mightiest most powerful king in the world." The king was impressed with the second answer.

"The third question," said the king, "Is the most important of the three. What would you do for me if I spared the life of your lovely bride?" Without hesitation, the mighty warrior humbly replied, "Sir, if you spared the life of my sweetheart I would die for you!"

The king was now touched. He not only offered freedom to the three, but he promised them a home in his kingdom, with servants and anything their hearts could desire. The warrior left the throne room with his wife and son.

Out on the palace steps the warrior turned to his bride to say, "Honey did you notice the gorgeous tapestry on the walls leading up to the king's throne?"

"No," she replied, "I didn't seem to notice that."

"Well, what did you think about that luxurious red and royal carpet that led up to the magnificent throne of the King?"

Again came the reply of the wife, "No, I really don't remember that either my prince," she quietly whispered.

"Surely," in frustration he said, "You noticed the precious gems, the diamonds and rubies, the gold and silver on that magnificent wall behind the king's throne?"

Again, "No," came the reply.

"My darling," said the warrior, almost spellbound, "How could you possibly miss the carpet, and the tapestry and even the untold wealth in stones and precious metals? At what in the world were you looking?" he begged.

"My loving husband," she softly spoke, "I could not take my eyes off the face of the man who said he would die for me."

Written words on a page cannot remotely capture the thrill of my life to realize that Jesus had done that for me. He had not only said He would die, but He literally died in my place so that I might live. He died on a cross between two thieves as He took all the sins of the world upon Him, for you and for me!

It was beyond my comprehension. My heroes of the sport's world proudly yet humbly said, "Jesus Christ is the most important person in my life."

They quoted the words of Paul who said in Romans 1:16, "I am not ashamed of the gospel, for it is the power of God for salvation to everyone who believes, to the Jew first and also to the Greek."

I really did not understand that, but if He was good enough for them, He was good enough for me! So, I simply invited Jesus Christ into my heart. That was the beginning of a life of **ENTHUSIASM**.

Later, I realized what all that meant to me personally. I realized *each of us has sinned* (or messed-up) *and has fallen short of what God created us to be* (Romans 3:23).

Because of that sin, or separation from God, *the penalty is death, or eternal separation from God* (Romans 6:23).

The Good News is that *while we were yet sinners, and separated from God, Christ died for you and for me that we might have life eternal* (Romans 5:8).

Jesus came that we might have an abundant life (John 10:10) here and now and He also promised us eternal life - forever with Him. "In my Father's house are many dwelling places prepared for you" (John 14).

Did you know that you and I may know these things and still miss it? Romans 10:9, 10 says, *"If we confess with our mouth and believe in our heart that Jesus Christ was raised from the dead, we shall be saved."* That means saved from a life of frustration and misery on earth, and saved from a life totally separated from God forever when we die. I certainly didn't want to miss-out on either of those free gifts! You and I must act now upon these truths.

What about this "Awesome Entrance?" Let me tell you why it is so totally awesome. The divine God, creator of the universe came to the earth as a man, Jesus Christ. That was pretty awesome in itself - when "the Word became flesh and dwelt among us" (John 1:14)... and many people witnessed that miracle.

The beyond human imagination, divine, magnificent, miraculous and totally awesome entrance to which I refer has been witnessed by many more - even more than those who saw Jesus Christ. This miracle has been witnessed by thousands and even millions of people who have been touched by the miraculous and awesome entrance of the Holy Spirit into their lives.

When God, through His Holy Spirit enters into your life or mine it happens in a supernatural way that defies human explanation. The Bible records the story of a man healed of his blindness. When questioned about his new found sight he simply replied, "All I know is once I was blind, now I can see!" He didn't need an explanation or a snap shot proof of the event. He simply experienced it. You and I have a similar, although perhaps dramatically different experience with the awesome entrance of the spirit of God into our own lives.

God does not care what shape the home of your heart is in when He arrives. When He makes His divine entrance into your heart and life He immediately begins to encourage and lift and enrich you, from the inside out. Remember, it's an inside job. The outside will take care of itself! The inner peace and joy that Jesus gives will explode into the warmth of a smile and a glow on the outside. The life of enthusiasm can radiate to those around you.

Will He make you a totally different person? Will you have to give-up all those favorite "things" you have enjoyed in the past? Maybe, maybe not! The Lord will bring things to your awareness that you may have never noticed. The music you've thrived on in the past may not be of much value to you in the future. The drink that you may have one day enjoyed may taste bitter to you from this day forward.

Your appetites may change in other ways as well. The materials you read, the movies you watched, the people you hang around, perhaps your thoughts will also change. In fact, that is the most important thing that will change! II Corinthians 5:17 says, "If any man is in Christ, he is a new creature; the old things passed away; behold, new things have come."

Initially, there may be a tugging on your old life before Christ came into your heart. He may inspire you to make some changes, as He changes your attitudes about certain things. As a little boy our young son Paul moved to a new school in third grade. He left all his friends he had been with for three years. It was an entirely new environment in every way. It took more and more of the new to forget about the old. The old was not necessarily bad, as in the case with his previous school. The old in your life may not have been all bad either - but it may not be the best for you.

The point is the new life in Christ is so much better. The **CREATOR** has taken-up residence in His Creation! That is the ideal, the perfect intention from the beginning! God created you and me to have fellowship with Him. That fellowship is created with His divine entrance into our lives.

You are special! God wants to come into your life and make you the best you can be. As we allow God to mold us and to make us into His perfect image, it may hurt at times as the rough edges are removed. Of course it hurts to "get-in-shape" for any new adventure.

The awesome entrance of God into your life will give you the power to be greater than you are. "He who is in you is greater than he who is in the world" (I John 4:4). Jesus told His disciples to wait until the Holy Spirit came to give them **POWER!** (Acts 1:8). Webster describes "awe" as to reverence, to fear, to wonder. Oh, what an awesome God we have!

One verse dramatically changed my life from one of frustration, although already a believer. Paul said in Galatians 2:20, *"I am crucified with Christ; and it is no longer I who live, but Christ lives in me; and the life which I now live in the flesh I live by faith in the Son of God, who loved me and delivered Himself up for me."*

As a Christian, it is no longer simply me struggling along trying to do the right things. It is Christ living His life through mine as I become more and more conscious of His presence, His thoughts and His personality in my life.

Many call this the "exchanged life." Christ exchanged His life for mine as He paid the penalty for my sin, as He bridged the gap of separation between God and me. Secondly, the Holy Spirit took up residence in my heart to make me the best of what God created me to be. God has blessed us "with every spiritual blessing in the heavenly places in Christ...He chose us in Him before the foundation of the world, that we should be holy and blameless before Him" (Ephesians 1). *"For by grace you have been saved through faith and that not of yourselves, it is the gift of God"* (Ephesians 2:8,9).

If you received a gift from someone, whether it was for Christmas, birthday or just a thank you, you would immediately open it. As I wrote these words, my wife Judy just came into my study to say, "I am going to open that birthday gift your Mom and Dad sent today!" She realized of course she had to wait...two more days until her birthday. The Dietzels never open gifts ahead of time (not my favorite tradition I might add!). She wanted to open it because she couldn't wait to find out what it was!

God's grace is a gift we need to unwrap and discover. Paul begins that unwrapping process for us in chapter three of Ephesians. Writing from jail, where he spent most of his time, Paul told us that God revealed a "mystery" to him that he enthusiastically wanted to share (Ephesians 3:3ff). He went on to tell us that God has "unfathomable riches in store for those who ask" (Ephesians 3:16). In modern day vernacular Paul said, "Don't worry about me guys...just because I'm in jail...God has a great deal for you!"

Paul prayed that *"He (God) would grant you, according to the riches of His glory to be strengthened with power through His Spirit in the inner man; so that Christ may dwell in your hearts through faith"* (Ephesians 3:17ff)..."*that you, being rooted and grounded in love, may be able to comprehend with all the saints what is the breadth and length and height and depth, to know the love of Christ which surpasses knowledge, that you may be filled up to all the fullness of God. Now to Him who is able to do exceedingly abundantly beyond all that we ask or think, according to the power that works within us."*

That is some heavy stuff! That's what I have been trying to let you in on in fact. If Christ is dwelling in our heart. If we have that Christ within, God within "Enthusiasm" - we can do "exceedingly abundantly beyond all that we ask or think" (Ephesians 3:20).

We are certainly convinced by now that it is not an outward motivation or circumstance that gives us hope and power. This is an "inside job." God has to do the living and working within our lives. How can that be? How can a supernatural, awesome and infinite God take up residence in my life or yours? Jesus told Nicodemus (John 3:3), *"Truly, truly, I say to you, unless man is born again, he cannot see the kingdom of God."* To be *"born again"* means to experience that awesome entrance of Jesus Christ into your life.

"The Lord works from the inside out. The world works from the outside in. The world would take people out of the slums. Christ takes the slums out of people, and then they take themselves out of the slums. The world would mold men by changing their environment. Christ changes men, who then change their environment. The world would shape human behavior, but Christ can change human nature." (Ezra Taft Benson)

We can't explain it, we can't understand it, we can only accept it as His special free gift to us. Again, one said it best..."Once I was blind...Now I can see!"

Read on...

Once I Was Blind - Now I See!

Upon a cross He bore the sins
Of the future lives of man;
Yet He smiled upon the ones he loved
As the nails pierced His hands.

In sweat of blood our Christ did hang,
While the steel ripped His skin
And faithless creatures stood below
And laughed and jeered at Him.

Now the path to celestial halls,
With tracks of blood did He leave
A blazoned trail, cleared for us -
If only we believe.

By faith we believe, all doubt is removed,
Life is abundant and free;
There's no explanation, but one said it all:
"Once I was blind...now I see!"

Stephen P. Dietzel

You Are What You Think You Are -

not!

The mind of man (woman implied also) is one of the most awesome tools in the hands of God Almighty. If we can somehow gain the mind of God, we will be able to handle every situation. *I am not actually what I think I am, but I am what I think!* I need to think God thoughts!

That is about as hard to grasp as it was as a child to figure out, "Who was here before God was here?" God was always here. He was here first. "But who was here before that?" God is the great "I AM" - He was here before here was here!

Proverbs 23:7 says of man, *"As he thinks within himself, so he is."* Think about it! I become what I think about. Again, I am not what I think I am, but I am what I think! Nothing is more important than my thoughts.

"Whatever is true, whatever is honorable, whatever is right, whatever

31

is pure, whatever is lovely, whatever is of good repute, if there is any excellence and if anything worthy of praise, let your mind dwell on these things" (Phil. 4:8).

Paul's joy would be made complete if he could somehow be like Christ. Paul said in Philippians 2:1, *"If therefore there is any encouragement in Christ, if there is any consolation of love, if there is any fellowship of the Spirit, if any affection and compassion, make my joy complete by being of the same mind, maintaining the same love, united in spirit, intent on one purpose."*

"Have this attitude in yourselves which was also in Christ Jesus" (Phil. 2:5). That attitude was **"ENTHUSIASM!"** Jesus, more than any man before or since had the God within, fullness of God on the inside of His life. You and I can have it too! Hold on, here we go on the journey!

Someone once said, "If you sow a thought, you reap an action; if you sow an action you reap a habit; if you sow a habit you reap a lifestyle; if you sow a lifestyle, you reap a destiny! One little thought begins as a tiny seed to sprout into one of life's greatest oaks.

"How blessed is the man who does not walk in the counsel of the wicked, nor stand in the path of sinners, nor sit in the seat of scoffers! But his delight is in the law of the Lord, and on His law he meditates day and night. And he will be like a tree firmly planted by streams of water, which yields its fruit in its season, and its leaf does not wither; and in whatever he does, he prospers" (Psalm 1:1-3).

What if we could somehow plug into that mind set? What if somehow we could program our minds and grow our minds to be like God. Forget all the positive thinking, and all the motivational tapes and books - let's learn to be like God! Let's start thinking His thoughts. Let's even dream of being like Him!

"I can do all things through Christ who strengthens me" (Philippians

4:13). Paul made that statement just after he had said in verse 12, *"I know how to get along with humble means, and I also know how to live in prosperity; in any and every circumstance I have learned the secret of being filled and going hungry, both of having abundance and suffering need."* He had said in verse 11, *"I have learned to be content in whatever circumstances I am."*

Paul strived to be like Christ. That was his goal, his aim in life to be more like Jesus. Paul must have dreamed in jail of one day being just like Jesus. Victor Frankel in his book Man's Search for Meaning, said, "Everything can be taken from a man but one: the last of the human freedoms - to choose one's attitude in any given set of circumstances, to choose one's own way."

No one can control your mind! No one can control your attitudes. The little school boy was told to sit down again and again. Finally he sat down, then he shouted, "I may be sitting down on the outside, but I'm standing-up on the inside!"

We quit dreaming and thinking and searching for more when we were like that little boy. We quit picturing the multicolored rainbows, and the yellow-brick roads, and the emerald cities. Now people live in only black and white colored square worlds wrapped in red tape.

Let's begin to really work on a Getting-Up Attitude! Bill Glass, former pro-football star who heads a fabulous prison ministry said, *"Getting-up* for the game is not a temporary emotional binge that you go on immediately before game time. *Getting-Up* is a whole way of life!"

"Getting up is a whole way of thinking that throws out negative pictures from your mind by replacing them with positive pictures of success." He went on to say, "You will play exactly as you see yourself play in your mind. If you burn the image of the person you want to become in your mind long enough, and vividly enough, you will

discover that you will become, over a period of time, what you see yourself being in your imagination."

Bill Glass didn't invent those thoughts, he just put them into useable language. For years and years the great motivators, the great thinkers, the tremendous leaders of all history have proclaimed the importance of our thoughts. Let's think some great thoughts, let's each dream of being someone special - for we are - you are!

Let's begin to dream beyond our day-to-day belief pattern. When we turned five or six years old we could really dream. Nobody held us back or knocked us down, we just dreamed! Guess what? Dreams are still for those of us who want to achieve more. If you haven't already "arrived" at your destination, begin to dream about it!

Remember your first "home" away from home? Maybe you are there now? If you're in an apartment, make what you have the neatest most comfortable apartment you can manage. Remember your first car? Mine was a '58 Volvo the summer of 1966 before my senior year in high school. I remember washing and waxing thinking my eight year old car looked like brand new. Make the best of what you have. Be the best you can be. Be happy with your best you!

At the same time, although we are content and happy, we do not need to be complacent. We can still strive to do more and be more and provide better for our families. We must believe we can be better today, so we will be better tomorrow. You aren't what you think you are, but what you think, you are!

God wants us to live abundantly. Jesus said in John 10:9-10, *"I am the door; if anyone enters through Me, he shall be saved, and shall go in and out, and find pasture. The thief comes to steal, and kill, and destroy; I came that they might have life, and might have it abundantly."* Notice, He came not to simply *show* us life, or to be a good example. He came that we might have life - the Spirit-filled life of enthusiasm.

All the good things of this life aren't reserved for the "other guys." Our concentration, however, is not on *things*, it is on seeking Him first, before the "things" can come. In Matthew 6:33-34 Jesus says, *Seek first His kingdom and His righteousness; and all these* things *shall be added to you* (my emphasis on "things"). . . *Therefore do not be anxious for tomorrow, for tomorrow will care of itself. Each day has enough trouble of its own."*

Guess what else? **ENTHUSIASM** is catchy. Other people get caught-up in your enthusiasm. The same is true with dreams. People like to follow someone who can really dream - especially when some of those dreams come true! Let's begin to dream about life as if everything depended upon those dreams. At the same time, let's begin to pray about everything as if it all depended upon God. When we can match our dreams with His dreams for us, then real excitement begins.

A fine evangelist, Manly Beasley was a man who consistently lived a life of faith. Perhaps the most powerful truths he lived by was on a plaque in his home, "Faith is believing a thing is so, before it is so, so it will be so!" In other words, you need to believe it before it happens so it will happen! You must first dream it, or visualize it - before it can happen! You must first be able to visualize your special dream home, car, boat or whatever goal it is that you really want to attain. In the world of athletics this belief is so important. "Winning is believing you have won before you have won, so you will win!"

You may or may not remember when I gave you a million dollars several chapters ago. You may have written a list of all the things for which you were going to use the money. Take that "million dollar dream list" and begin to arrange the items in priority order. List in numerical order the things that are most important to you. You might also divide your list into different categories, many motivators suggest physical, mental, spiritual and social.

Man did not think-up those four categories either. Luke 2:52 tells us that, *"Jesus kept increasing in wisdom and stature, and in favor with God and men."* He had been in His Father's house, worshiping His heavenly Father. A natural result of that relationship with His Father was growth. Let's categorize our dream list beginning with those same four areas: physical, mental, our relationships with God (spiritual) and man (social). You may also decide to add business, financial, retirement planning, and others - nobody cares more about you than YOU - so you plan the important areas of your life.

"Awesome Entrance?" Remember what is really important here! Your dreams and your goals, the target for which you aim in this great adventure of life needs to be checked through the divine filter of God's Word. Is your dream, goal or idea one that will be good for your relationship with God? Will it be good for your relationship with other people? Do you really deep down inside believe in your dreams? If not, they will become useless daydreams.

Are your dreams inspired by **ENTHUSIASM**, a God within inspiration? Do you really know for sure it is Him in your life, and not you? Don't base your knowledge on feelings, base it upon facts. We need to **KNOW** for sure that we **KNOW HIM!**

Read on....

Parable of the Wristband

Four touchdowns they scored and the big game they won,
The star gave his wristband to my proud little son.

He washed it to wear it so that others might know,
That he had the wristband from his quarterback hero.

A hero and a wristband, it gave him such pride,
But my son knows another in his heart - down inside.

For another gave a wristband - as God said in His Word,
This is the record - so you know what you've heard.

Life eternal is my gift, if you know My Son;
Yet with Jesus, not a ball game but a life you have won!

Stephen P. Dietzel

I KNOW THAT I KNOW AN AWESOME GOD!

"This is the testimony, that God has given us eternal life, and this life is in His Son. He who has the Son has life; and he who has not the Son of God has not life. These things have I written unto you that believe on the name of the Son of God, that you may KNOW you have eternal life..." (I John 5:11-13)

Enthusiasm is an inside job provided by the totally awesome entrance of Jesus Christ into our lives. As He begins to motivate our thoughts, new habits are formed. New habits create lifestyle changes that ultimately will effect our destiny. Since that God-given, God-within enthusiasm is so important, it surely would be assuring to KNOW that I have it!"

One of the most asked questions of believers today is, "How do you know that you really **KNOW** God?" John tells us (1 John 5:13), *"I have written these things...that you may know that you have eternal life."* He uses the word "**KNOW**" thirty-eight times in that short epistle.

The Gospel of John was written "that you might have life." Jesus said, *"I have come that you might have life and have it more abundantly, that it might be full and meaningful"* (John 10:10). The epistle of John (I John) was written that we might **KNOW** we have life. It is important enough to repeat again, *"This is the record, God has given us eternal life and the life is in the Son; He who has the Son has life, he who has not the Son of God has not life, these things have I written to you that you might know you have everlasting life"* (I John 5:10). We have an "I KNOW SO," not an "I hope so" faith!

Whenever you begin to doubt or wonder about your relationship with God, or doubt your "salvation" read the entire book of I John. In fact, if you read this little five-chapter book every day for a month it will become part of your life. My favorite book in the Bible is the book of I John - I know it!

In I John 5:1, we see the first evidence of "Knowing God." We must have a **DEFINITE EXPERIENCE** with Jesus Christ. At some point in time, although we may not know the exact day or hour, we still know that moment when we had a definite experience.

Let me tell you how that may have happened for you. You were going along in life, doing your own thing when you realized God wanted to really make a difference in your life.

Realize this - God is in the life-changing business. He really does want you and me to live life to its fullest. Even though we each have to have a definite life-changing experience, the **INCIDENTALS** may change in every life. Don't try to have someone else's "life-changing experience."

Remember the awesome report from the blind man: "Once I was blind, but now I see!" There were at least three on record in the Bible without sight. They each had a unique story to tell. One blind man asked to be healed and Jesus simply spoke the words, "Be healed." He was given his sight. For a second blind man Jesus rubbed some spittle and dirt together and rubbed it on the man's eyes - and he could see. For a third blind man Jesus only touched his eyes and his sight was restored.

Which man was healed? Which man received his sight? ALL three men were changed in an instant! You could not doubt any one of them. At the same time, if you have had a definite experience with Jesus Christ, although some may doubt you no one can deny the reality of your experience.

Once you have had a definite experience with Jesus Christ there are other evidences in your life of "knowing Him." You will have an internal witness of the Spirit in your life. It is not simply an emotional moment, but is a reality in your life. I John 5:10 says, *"The one who believes in the Son of God has the witness in himself."* He goes on to say in I John 4:13, *"By this we know that we abide in Him and He in us, because He has given us of His Spirit."*

As a college athlete it seemed many others around me had had a "real experience" with God that was foreign to me. There was the boy running around the track who was struck in the back of the leg by a javelin. It ripped through his skin and protruded through the other side of his leg.

In that instant of pain and fear my friend told the Lord he would serve him forever if God would heal him. What a unique experience! I was certainly glad it was his experience and not my own!

Then there was the drug addict in one of my college courses. He really was a wild one! He was involved in everything, but definitely in the other crowd from me. Then there was a change in his life. He came to know Jesus Christ in a personal way through the ministry of Campus Crusade for Christ. It was not a gradual change, it was immediate, it was in an instant. He became a radical for Jesus. Like the apostle Paul, he totally changed!

We've all heard of the highly dramatic experiences of those who traded drugs, or wealth or fame for a relationship with God, but how about the normal guy or gal? How about the person who grew-up pretty straight without carrying a lot of bad baggage? How about you?

As a nine year old, theology was certainly not one of my strong points, but I know this - I knew Him! I knew I had had a definite experience with the man called Jesus. The peace I had as a youth was much like the safety and security you feel when you walk hand in hand with your father, or someone you love and trust. You don't worry about falling when that special person has your hand.

The Psalmist lifted his eyes to the Lord in hope and praise in Psalm 73, especially in verses 23-28: *"I am continually with Thee; Thou has taken hold of my right hand. With Thy counsel Thou wilt guide me, and afterward receive me to glory. Who have I in heaven but Thee? And besides Thee, I desire nothing on earth...God is the strength of my heart and my portion forever...the Lord God is my refuge, that I may tell of all Thy works."* Notice again, God is holding your "right" hand! He won't let you down, for you really "are in good hands!" Remember the song, "Put your hand in the hand of the man from Galilee?" Praise the Lord!

"Trust in the Lord with all your heart, and do not lean on your own understanding. In all your ways acknowledge Him, and He will make your paths straight" (Proverbs 3:5,6).

We are not born into Christianity. We don't inherit or earn it. Before we have that awesome relationship our awareness of spiritual things is minimal. Once the Heavenly Father makes that divine contact we are never the same. Do you remember the times before that awesome entrance? We echo the words of the apostle Paul, as he said in Philippians 3:13-14, *"one thing I do: forgetting about things behind and reaching forward to what lies ahead, I press on toward the goal for the prize of the upward call of God in Christ Jesus."*

We do not want to dwell on the past, we simply want to learn from it. Life is a series of learning experiences, if we're looking to learn! *"Since we are surrounded by so great a cloud of witnesses, let us lay aside every weight, and the sin which so easily ensnares us, and let us run with endurance the race that is set before us, looking unto Jesus, the author and finisher of our faith, who for the joy that was set before Him endured the cross..."* (Hebrews 12:1,2).

As we allow God to mold our hearts and our minds, that transformation will produce all the other necessary changes we need. Don't let the "crabs" of life pull you down! If you put several crabs into a bucket you don't need a lid. Why? When one crab starts to climb out, one or more of the other crabs will pull him down, back into the bucket. Have you ever been there? You have tried to climb up or out of your possibly sad circumstances, only to get pulled back down by your "friends" or family?

Concentrate on the good things, the positive and uplifting things about your life. Climb above those that try to "protect" you from possible failures. Remember, failing is not just falling - failing is not getting up when you fall!

TODAY IS THE DAY! Now is the time! There is no better time than now to adopt a lifestyle of enthusiasm - for His glory! Begin today to make a difference in the lives of everyone about you. Let enthusiasm get hold of your life. Let the Holy Spirit of God release His awesome power in your life. Live life to its fullest **TODAY!**

Read on...

Live For Today!

TOMORROW and tomorrow and tomorrow
Is the day of hopes and dreams;
But when we live for tomorrow alone
Today becomes less it seems.

TODAY is the day in which we must live
To enjoy the fruit of the land;
When life is fresh and our spirits new,
The time to be is at hand.

So why relive the days that have past,
Or wish for the ones far ahead;
Freedom and abundance are present now
So live TODAY instead.

God is waiting to come into your heart,
He'll enter if you will allow,
And transform your life abundant and full;
The time is TODAY - it is NOW!!!

Stephen P. Dietzel

Lost Treasure? I Found It!

One of these **TOTALLY AWESOME** books, like you have in your hands, has three Delta airline tickets in the back. These tickets are transferable and good anytime in the next year to fly first class to the destination of your choice. Turn quickly and see if the tickets are in your book.

The fact is, there honestly were three round trip tickets in the back of this book as I wrote it in the fall of 1994. They belonged to my sweetheart Judy, my son Paul and me. We had been on a fiftieth wedding anniversary celebration ski trip with my parents in April. When the plane was over booked, we gladly volunteered to "give-up our seats." In case you were not aware of this program, check with the airlines.

We love to travel during holidays and busy times of the year in hopes of "giving-up our seats." The reward for the slight inconvenience is often round-trip tickets to the destination of your choice! Several years ago we enjoyed a free trip to San Francisco with my parents. Two years ago my Dad and I enjoyed a ski trip to Alta, Utah - free and fabulous! My family is planning another ski trip next February - on our first class tickets from the last ski trip!

Now, here is the point. Because you didn't really have the tickets in the back of your book, you were not overly disappointed when you found the back cover empty. On the other hand, if you had placed **YOUR** tickets there for safekeeping and realized you lost them - you would be very much disappointed! If you have ever been unfortunate enough to lose something of value you understand.

All of us have lost things, but have **YOU** ever been lost? As a little boy I often wondered off on a mountain path in West Point, New York where my dad coached Army or the United States Military Academy. The trail was less than a mile from my home, although it seemed to like hundreds of miles that one day. The warm Sunday morning sunshine is still as fresh in my mind as when I first started down the trail. I was cool and cocky, whistling along free as a lark. I was lost for perhaps an hour, but I wasn't nervous for I didn't know I was lost! However, at the split second I realized my lost condition, fear overcame me.

As a little boy of seven I remember the tears streaming down my cheeks. I remember distinctly the horror and the emptiness as I realized I really was lost with no way home. Walking down one path then another I screamed for help. Surely someone would hear me.

After what seemed like hours, suddenly I noticed a small clearing through the blur of my teary eyes. In the distance I could faintly but surely see home! What a sudden relief. What a tremendous lift and encouragement it was to be safe at last. Just to see our familiar house was the comfort I needed - even though it was still a long way away.

When we are "lost" and away from God we are often carefree and without concern for spiritual things. As long as no major problems come up we seem to move along through life with little turmoil. All that changes when we realize we are lost, and separate from

God - when we realize He may be the only "out" or solution to our monumental problem. It often takes a catastrophe to bring us to the reality of knowing we need help from someone much bigger than ourselves.

Interestingly enough we remain in that lost and so lonely position of separation until we somehow are struck with the reality of God. At that moment we "find God" our cares seem to vanish. We still may have problems and circumstances beyond our comprehension, but we have a "caretaker" or better yet a "caregiver" who lifts our burdens of life, if we only let Him.

What a thrill to see home, to realize He has a special plan and a prepared place for each of us in life. How do I know? Because that still small voice within says, *"This is the way, walk in it"* (Isaiah 30:21). Jesus says, *"I am the way, the truth and the life. No man comes to the Father except through me"* (John 14:6). You just know that you know!

You have a peace that passes all understanding. You can with confidence believe Proverb 3:5 that says, *"Trust in the Lord with all your heart, lean not on your own understanding; in all your ways acknowledge Him and He shall make your path straight."* You will never again be "lost" in the everlasting presence of God. Believe it. Take comfort in that fact. Act upon it. Do it now!

Not only can you **KNOW** that you know Him, but once you are in the family of God you are in forever! Jesus says, *"I'll never leave you nor forsake you"* (Hebrews 13:5). The Father has taken hold of your right hand (Psalm 73:23). You may lose your grip and slip, but, the Heavenly Father will not lose you!

In John 10:25ff, Jesus talks about His eternal relationship with His sheep. *"I told you, and you do not believe; the works that I do in My Father's name, these bear witness of Me. But you do not believe, because you are not My sheep. My sheep hear My voice, and I know them, and they follow Me; and I give eternal life to them, and they shall never perish; and no one shall snatch them out of My hand."*

What a thrill to know that if you and I are His sheep, we are forever in the flock! God wants us to have the comfort, the peace and the assurance of knowing we are his children - forever. If one who seemingly was a sheep is now away from the fold, perhaps he was merely a wolf in sheep's clothes. On the other hand, a true sheep can only be "temporarily" lost from the shepherd.

God is in control. *"The Lord is not slow about His promise, as some count slowness, but is patient toward you, not wishing for any to perish but for all to come to repentance"* (II Peter 3:9).

God really can and will make each of us champions in life. He will protect us in the trials and tribulations of life. Do you remember "**CHAMP?**" He will lift us and carry us through the challenges. Our "help" comes from the Lord in the midst of trouble. The internal and eternal enthusiasm gained by His awesome entrance into our lives enables you and me to provide "maximum effort." As a "child of the King" the eternal price for us has been paid.

"The joy of the Lord is my strength!" If you don't have joy in your life today, something is wrong with that God within, Holy Spirit led enthusiasm in your life. Once you are His child nothing will ever change that fact. You may change your name and move out of the country, but you cannot move out of the family.

Perhaps you know someone that once seemed so close to the Lord, but now they seem lost and far away. Chances are that person never really knew the Lord. If they sincerely knew my Lord, they would never want to be anywhere but in His precious family. You see, once you have had the taste of heaven on earth, the abundant life that Jesus gives the believer, you will never want to lose it!

Go back to the fantastic book of I John. Again, the gospel of John was written so we might have life. The epistle of I John was written that we might **KNOW** what we have in Christ. The book of I John gives us the "evidences" of our relationship with Christ. Again, spend a month with I John then move to another of Paul's exciting books - enjoy "every Spiritual blessing" in Ephesians.

As I write this book I am reminded of a commitment I made to myself years ago to memorize I John. It is so valuable to you and to me as Christians. Let's look at the highlights together as we wrap up the **TOTALLY AWESOME** relationship we can have with Him.

The gospel of John begins with one of my favorite passages in the scriptures. This is a definite memory verse if you are serious about your relationship with the Lord. *"In the beginning was the Word, and the Word was with God, and the Word was God. He was in the beginning with God. All things came into being by Him, and apart from Him nothing came into being that was come into being. In Him was life, and the life was the light of men. And the light shines in the darkness, and the darkness did not comprehend it"* (John 1:1-5).

Very simply that passage says *"the Word was with God, and the Word was God."* If the Word is God, and you and I want to get to know God, then we need to get to know His Word!

Here is my question to you (and to me). If you spend as much time in His Word the next ten years as you have the last ten years will you know Him any better? If you continue growing in your relationship like you have been growing - are you growing? We must do more in the future than we have in the past, or more time will pass - wasted!

The sad testimony is this. People on the outside of our churches don't really want to possess anything they see on the inside, because they see nothing different than what they already have. They already experience fear, doubt, frustration, and lack of joy and purpose in their lives. If there is nothing in the storehouse, then we may as well not put anything in the showcase! The time has come for you and me to be so possessed by the life of Christ that others just have to get caught-up in the enthusiasm!

Let's get back to I John. For those who may say, "I don't have the natural enthusiasm you have...I am not outgoing...I am not articulate... I am not knowledgeable about spiritual things...I cannot share my faith." You are not sharing your faith for one of two reasons, and two alone. Number one, you don't have a relationship to share...or, number two you really don't **KNOW** what you have in Christ. This is for you!

We need to know this..."*What was from the beginning, what we have heard, what we have seen with our eyes, what we beheld and our hands handled, concerning the Word of Life - the life was manifested and we have seen and bear witness and proclaim to you the eternal life... what we have seen and heard we proclaim to you also that you also may have fellowship with us...*" (I John 1:1ff) He goes on to say in verse four, "*these things we write, so that our joy may be made complete.*"

Did you catch that? All John and the other guys were doing is telling others (like you and me!) what they had "heard" and "seen" with their own ears and eyes. Like the blind men who were healed, they simply said, "Once I was blind, now I see." They didn't need a seminary degree, or a Biblical education, they simply needed an experience with the living God. Have you had that experience? If not, it is not too late...but time is passing by quickly.

John went on to share another of my favorite verses in the entire Bible. I John 1:5 says, "*This is the message we have heard from Him and announce to you, that God is light, and in Him there is no darkness at all. If we say that we have fellowship with Him and yet walk in the darkness, we lie and do not practice the truth, but if we walk in the light as He Himself is in the light, we have fellowship with one another, and the blood of Jesus His Son cleanses us from all sin. If we say we have no sin, we are deceiving ourselves, and the truth is not in us. If we confess our sins, He is faithful and righteous to forgive us our sins and to cleanse us from all unrighteousness."*

That is enough truth to carry you and me through any storm of life! God is light - there's no darkness in Him. We need to get in the light and soak-up the heavenly rays of His Holy Word! When we walk in the light, we walk in the hope of Jesus. We walk with a spirit of **ENTHUSIASM** that is infectious. God gives you a charisma about your life that is beyond human explanation.

As I write this chapter it is after midnight and quiet and dark in the rest of the house. As I walk into the bedroom in a little while there is a really good chance I will stub my toe on a chair, or run into the wall - if I leave the lights off! In darkness, it is tough to get around. Light is the great revealer of the path ahead.

At the same time, as the lights are low in my study everything looks orderly and in place with pictures hung perfectly straight and with no imperfections on the walls or carpet. As I turn the lights up brighter I realize again that there are papers and books everywhere and the trash can is overflowing. It is also readily evident to me that there are several nicks in the paint and a scrape where I backed my chair into the wall behind my desk. These imperfections are noticeable as the light becomes brighter and brighter. The light reveals blemishes that may need correction - as we seek perfection..."*you shall be perfect as your Father in heaven is perfect"* (Matthew 5:48).

Our lives are like that. As we bring more and more light, the light of God's Word, into our lives He makes us aware of dark and "dangerous" areas that are hazardous to our health. As we bring our thought life under His control, as we think on positive and uplifting truths from His Word we have the peace and the joy that are to be the norms of the Christian life. We are to use the revealing light to mold us and make us more like Jesus. Again, *"You shall be perfect as your Father in heaven is perfect* (Matthew 5:48). We will never receive "sinless perfection" on this earth - but we are to strive to be like Jesus.

When you have a close personal relationship with someone, you tend to want to please that person. You enjoy doing what the other person enjoys doing. You like to be together with someone you care about. I John 2:15 says, *"Do not love the world or the things of the world. If anyone loves the world, the love of the Father is not in him."* Chapter 3:7,8 goes on to say, *"Little children, let no one deceive you, the one who practices righteousness is righteous, just as He is righteous; the one who practices sin is of the devil..."*

The tense used in the Greek for "practices" righteousness is a continuing action. It means the one who continues to practice. If we practice the presence of God, if we practice "right" things, then we will grow in a "right" relationship with Him. If we practice wrong things, sinful things, which are separate and opposed to and apart from the ways of God, we will be miserable. When we know what is right, yet do wrong we have a guilty conscious and a defeated spirit. When we practice "right things" our life is filled with joy and abundance.

As we "practice the presence" of God, as we spend time in our relationship with Him we really enjoy doing what is right and hate doing what is wrong. We don't practice righteousness or right doing because of rules. We practice "right-living" because of the love relationship. We honestly want to do certain things because we want to do so, not because we are "required" to change. The joy of the Lord is our strength.

John goes on to tell us that we have a burden to tell other people about the relationship, about the "God within" **ENTHUSIASM** we have discovered (I John 5:19). You also have a real love and caring for other people, especially others in the kingdom of God (I John 4:7,8)..."*Love one another, for love is from God.*"

Like building any relationship, you will want to spend time with your new family, the Church of God, His people. You will want to spend time reading and studying His Word, the Bible. You will realize the Bible is a one-of-a-kind world's best seller...like a pool, shallow enough for a child to wade at its edge, yet, deep enough for an elephant to swim in the middle without touching bottom! What an awesome book! What an Awesome God!

One other thought...do you feel any differently? Some people do, others do not. The key point is this: do not worry about feelings. Depend upon the fact of God's Word. Remember I John 5:13, "*These things I have written...so you might* **KNOW** *you have everlasting life.*" You don't have to wish for it, or wonder about it, eternal life is yours if you Know Him. Mark it down. It's finished - it's a done deal - Forever!

Growing-up by the gridiron it still rings in my ears, "Fourth Quarter's Ours!" In athletic terms, particularly football, that means our team is in control of the last quarter of the contest. The leader for three quarters never reaches the record book, and will be remembered no more. That point was again brought to my attention in the fall of 1994 and the LSU - Auburn football game. Auburn had won fourteen games in a row. LSU had won very few of the last fourteen games!

At half-time, LSU lead by a score of 10-7. The score again changed several times in the second half...10-9...17-9...23-9...23-16...23-23... then 26-23! With just under two minutes to play, after Auburn had intercepted and had returned two passes for touchdowns...they did it again! Final score: LSU 26 - Auburn 30.

No one will remember the spectacular start, or even the miraculous middle quarters. At the fourth-quarter final gun the points on the scoreboard tell the only story that will last. "Auburn squeaks by the Tigers!"

Three quarters of Totally Awesome is over. It is my prayer and hope that these words have been a blessing to you. The Gospel message is certainly a message of **ENTHUSIASM**! It is the message of the mountaintop, even when you find yourself temporarily in the valley. Act upon what you know to be true. Live in victory.

Remember this, *"You shall know the truth, and the truth will set you free."* (John 8:32) "The world didn't give it, so the world can't take it away!" Where we find the truth is not as important as how we live it when we find it! Believe it's so before it's so, so it'll be so!" "Greater is He that is in you than He that is in the world!"

"There's an old Hindu legend," says Claude Bragdon, "that at one time all men on earth were gods, but that men so sinned and abused the Divine that Brahma, the god of all gods decided that the godhead should be taken away from man and hid some place where he would never again find it to abuse it. "We will bury it deep in the earth," said the other gods. "No," said Brahma, "because man will dig down in the earth and find it."

"Then we will sink it in the deepest ocean," they said. "No," said Brahma,"because man will learn to find it there too." "We will hide it on the highest mountain," they said. "No," said Brahma, "because man will someday climb every mountain on the earth and again capture the godhead."

"Then we do not know where to hide it where he cannot find it," said the lessor gods. "I will tell you," said Brahma, "hide it down in man himself. He will never think to look there." Brahma in this

Hindu legend assumed that man cannot have a personal and internal relationship with "the godhead." As Christians we realize that personal internal relationship is the only available through "the Christ" not a "godhead" but God Himself. Jesus said, *"I am the way, the truth and the life, no man comes to the Father but through me."*

Hidden down within each of our lives is a seed that God has planted at our birth – for we are created in God's image. That seed can be nourished in the warmth of His presence to bring us into His great forever family. We can neglect the seed, and the still small voice of God that speaks to our heart, or we can by faith respond. The *totally awesome* is available today - it is within - it is "An Theos" - **ENTHUSIASM!** It is for you!

Again, Jesus came that you might have life! He did not simply come to point the way, or show a sign, or challenge the champion. He came so you might have all the fullness of His Father...so that you and I might be like Him! He came because He is the way, the truth and the life. As believers, you and I are to be light, and salt, and to be truth.

No contrast in the Bible is more dramatic than light and darkness. We see the comparison between good and evil, God and Satan, heaven and hell, spiritual and fleshly, and on and on. As dramatically different as all those similarities may be, light and darkness shines as the greatest contrast. We may see light, we may use it, we certainly benefit by it in many ways, but there is much more. We, you and I, are called to be light. We are to be salt. We are to make a difference in our world!

A young lad who held a baby bird in his hands approached a wise man. The boy planned to trick the wise man with his well-thought-out question, "Mighty wise man, is the bird alive, or is it dead?" He knew if the man said, "Alive," he could crush the bird to death. If the response came back, "Dead," he would open his hands and let the bird fly away. With only a moment of thought the wise man quietly and patiently smiled saying, "It is as you wish my son."

The life of abundance and enthusiasm within is truly and totally awesome, but, it is totally up to you. Let "The Touch of the Master's Hand" change your life from the inside out. You will **NEVER** be the same!

The Touch of the Master's Hand

"Twas battered and scared, and the auctioneer
Thought it scarcely worth his while
To waste much time on the old violin,
But he held it up with a smile.
"What am I bid, good folks," he cried,
"Who'll start the bidding for me?
A dollar, a dollar - now who'll make it two -
Two dollars, and who'll make it three?

"Three dollars once, three dollars twice,
Going for three" - but no!
From the room far back a gray-haired man
Came forward and picked up the bow;
Then wiping the dust from the old violin,
And tightening up the strings,
He played a melody, pure and sweet,
As sweet as the caroling angel sings.
The music ceased and the auctioneer

With a voice that was quiet and low,
Said: "What am I bid for the old violin?"
And he held it up with the bow;
"A thousand dollars - and who'll make it two?
Two thousand - and who'll make it three?
Three thousand once, three thousand twice
And going - and gone," said he.

The people cheered, but some of them cried,
"We do not quite understand -
What changed its worth?" The man replied:
"The touch of the MASTER'S hand."
And many a man with life out of tune,
And battered and torn with sin,
Is auctioned cheap to a thoughtless crowd.
Much like the old violin.

A "mess of pottage," a glass of wine,
A game and he travels on,
He's going once, and going twice -
He's going - and almost gone!
But the MASTER comes, and the foolish crowd,
Never can quite understand,
The worth of a soul, and the change that is wrought
By the touch of the MASTER'S hand.

Myra Brook Welch

Back To Basics...

A ball, a bat, a balance beam,
A net, pit, pool or goal,
The Coach who stands above the rest
Looks past the court to the soul.

The competitor's focus is on the game,
Upon the fields of strife;
The Coach can see beyond the ball -
His chief concern is life.

The sights and sounds of victory filled the air. The proud Coach was carried from the arena on the shoulders of an exuberant team. Many hours, weeks, months and even years of training had produced the desired result. As the jubilant teammates entered the locker room, the electricity continued to flow.

Suddenly, the emotion of the moment changed. A hush covered the room as one by one, with head bowed, each athlete gently dropped to his knees. The silence was broken as the Coach humbly spoke to one greater than he, "Our Heavenly Father, we are grateful for the joy of this occasion. We thank you for the lessons of life you teach us through athletic competition. Help each of us remember whom we represent. Enable each of us to reach our full potential."

Few people have the platform enjoyed by the Coach. The Coach has the opportunity to point to a "still more excellent way" - **JESUS CHRIST.** You can know everything about God, but, not KNOW God. Until you know Him in an intimate and personal way, you are only the spectator in the game called life.

TO KNOW GOD you must take several steps:

ADMIT you are a sinner. *"For all have sinned and fall short of the glory of God"* (Romans 3:23).

ASK Christ into your life. *"Behold, I stand at the door and knock, if anyone hears My voice and opens the door, I will come in to him"* (Revelation 3:20).

ACKNOWLEDGE Him as Lord of your life. *"If you confess with your mouth Jesus as Lord, and believe in your heart that God raised Him from the dead, you shall be saved"* (Romans 10:9).

APPROACH the Word of God with a real hunger for right living. *"Blessed are those who hunger and thirst for righteousness, for they shall be satisfied"* (Matthew 5:6).

ABIDE in Him. *"If you abide in me and my words abide in you, ask whatever you wish, and it shall be done for you."* (John 15:7)

A GOOD COACH is a master of the basics. His teams make few mistakes because they do the common things uncommonly well. There is time for the spectacular...because the common, the basics, are habits of practice.

As the basics of the Bible become part of your daily life, God's ways will become your ways, His thoughts your thoughts. That will take time. Study the Bible one book, one chapter several verses at a time. Read a book generally, devotionally the first time, taking several days for longer books. Then, break the passage down to portions you can handle easily.

Read the passage as if you were the author, or first reader. Ask yourself several questions:

WHAT? What are the main thoughts and the key verses?

WHY? Why was the passage written?

HOW? How does the passage affect me today?

NATIONAL CHAMPIONSHIP? Few coaches have had the honor of being chosen Coach of the Year. Fewer still have had undefeated and untied National Championship seasons. No coach or team has reached that pinnacle of success without first mastering the fundamentals.

As you master the fundamentals of Bible study, God's Word will mean more and more to you. You will desire an even deeper walk with the Lord and will see great results.

PROSPERITY - *"Blessed is the man who does not walk in the counsel of the wicked...but his delight is in the Lord and in His law he meditates day and night...and in whatever he does, he prospers"* (Psalm 1:1-3).

PURITY - *"How can a young man keep his way pure? By keeping it according to Thy Word...Thy Word have I treasured in my heart that I may not sin against Thee"* (Psalm 119:9-11).

POWER - *"For I am not ashamed of the gospel, for it is the power of God for salvation to everyone who believes"* (Romans 1:16).

PEACE - *"The peace of God, which surpasses all comprehension, shall guard your hearts and minds in Christ Jesus"* (Philippians 4:7).

BEGIN YOUR GAME PLAN with the Gospel of John. Spend the first week reviewing the entire book by reading three chapters each day. On the eighth day, reread chapter one and ask yourself **"WHAT? WHY? HOW** does this affect me?"** Study a new chapter each day, writing down your thoughts. In just 28 days you will complete your study in John.

In the weeks following, study I John (week 5), James (week 6), Ephesians, Philippians, Romans, I Corinthians, etc., just as you have studied John. Look up key words in an English dictionary and a Bible dictionary. A concordance is also a helpful book for further study, as are Bible commentaries.

Read and study at your own pace. Do not make it a chore you regret, rather, let it become a habit you enjoy. This plan is only a guide, but there is no better time to begin than now.

No great coach, no great athlete ever achieved success in any contest until he first entered the contest. *"Be doers of the Word and not merely hearers"* (James 1:22).

What is your motivation for living? Who is your "Coach?" Who leads your life? Make the decision today that hundreds of thousands across America have made. Join His team in the game of life! Let that inner enthusiasm, that God within attitude be your motivator in life.

There's no better time to begin than now. Today's the Day!

Enthusiasm Makes the Difference!

Think on These Things!

BELIEVE YOU CAN SUCCEED AND YOU WILL! When little people try to drive you down - THINK BIG! When that 'I haven't got what it takes' feeling creeps upon you - THINK BIG! When an argument or quarrel seems inevitable - THINK BIG! When romance starts to slip - THINK BIG! When you feel your progress on the job is slowing down - THINK BIG!" (David Schwartz)

YOUR SUCCESS AND HAPPINESS START WITH YOU! You already have the ability necessary for success; man was designed for accomplishment, engineered for success and endowed with the seeds of greatness. In your hands you hold the seeds of failure or the potential for greatness." (Zig Zigler)

Stephen P. Dietzel

LEARN FROM SUCCESSFUL FAILURES: Babe Ruth struck-out more times than anyone in baseball. Hank Aaron who broke Ruth's record, struck out more than 99% of the players in the major leagues. Vince Lombardi, the most revered coach since Knute Rockne, yet, at 43 was only a line coach at Fordham University. Albert Einstein and Werner von Braun flunked courses in math! The only difference between a big shot and a little shot is the big shot is just a little shot who kept shooting." (Zig Zigler)

RESOURCES AND POWERS ARE GIVEN TO THOSE WHO USE what resources and powers they have. Through the use of our muscles, our muscles grow and harden. Through the use of our mind, mental capacity increases; through the use of our spiritual powers these powers heighten. We do not wear-out the mind with thinking, or the soul with loving and showing mercy." (Dr. Jay T. Stocking)

CONSIDER A PAINTING BY REMBRANDT or a bronze by Degas or a violin by Stradivarius or a play by Shakespeare. They have great value for two reasons: their creators were masters and they are few in number. Yet there are more than one of each of these. Never, in all seventy billion humans who have walked this planet since the beginning of time has there been anyone exactly like you!" (Og Mandino)

WEALTH, NOTORIETY, PLACE AND POWER are no measure of success whatever. The only true measure of success is the ratio between what we might have done and what we might have been on one hand, and the thing we have made and the thing we have made of ourselves on the other." (H.G. Wells)

IT IS A TRAGEDY indeed to see an ambitious person striving after some goal he has neither the energy nor ability to reach. But it is a thousand times greater tragedy and, alas, a more common one, to see Generals and Vice-Presidents, spiritual and mental leaders, passing by unnoticed as street car conductors, section hands, and bell-hops." (Robert Danforth)

PERSONALITY IS AN ILLUSIVE THING. Good looks, good habits, good education, fine family, magnificent supply of the best of life to draw from, and yet something lacking in the connections...some people have so much to give, but never give. (Robert Danforth)

"DO YOU FEEL" the world is treating you well? If your attitude toward the world is excellent, you will receive excellent results. If you feel so-so about the world, your response from that world will be average. Feel badly about your world, and you will seem to have only negative feedback from life." (John Maxwell)

SUCCESS IS TO LAUGH OFTEN AND MUCH; to win the respect of intelligent people and the affection of children; to earn the appreciation of honest critics and endure the betrayal of false friends; to appreciate beauty, to find the best in others; to leave the world a bit better, whether by a healthy child, a garden patch or a redeemed social condition; to know even one life has breathed easier because you have lived. This is to have succeeded. (Ralph Waldo Emerson)

ONE NEVER KNOWS WHAT HE MIGHT ACCOMPLISH until he tries. Give things a chance to happen! Give success a chance to happen! It is impossible to win the race unless you venture to run, impossible to win the victory unless you dare to battle." (Rich Devos)

DECIDE WHAT YOU WANT & WRITE DOWN YOUR GOALS. Then convert your goals into positive, present tense statements called affirmations. Affirm your goals each day until they become part of your subconscious mechanism. 'As a man thinketh, so is he.' If you are not making the progress you would like to make and are capable of making, it is simply because your goals are not clearly defined. (Paul Meyer)

SUPERSELF: There's a You inside of you that you may not have discovered or experienced yet - at least not on a continuous basis. It's the You able to achieve more than you ever imagined. It's the You able to make a personal or business plan and stick to it, bringing it in on time and on budget with no need for praise or accolades from anyone, just for the satisfaction of knowing that once you think it, you can do it. It's the You who welcomes new challenges with zest instead of intrepidation; who deals with the inevitable loss of a job, money, or someone close as a natural part of life instead of a devastating problem or some kind of punishment. It is You in control of life instead of being controlled by circumstances, events, children, bosses, parents, and plain old fear." (Charles Givens)and again...

THE OPTIMIST CREED: Promise Yourself - "To be so strong that nothing can disturb your peace of mind.* "To talk health, happiness and prosperity to every person you meet.* "To make all your friends feel that there is something in them.* "To look at the sunny side of everything and make your optimism come true.* "To think only of the best, to work only for the best and expect only the best.* "To be just as enthusiastic about the success of others as you are about your own.* "To forget the mistakes of the past and press on to the greater achievements of the future.* "To wear a cheerful countenance at all times and give every living creature you meet a smile.* "To give so much time to the improvement of yourself that you have no time to criticize others.* "To be too large for worry, too noble for anger, too strong for fear, and too happy to permit the presence of trouble."

Optimist International

THE MAN
WHO THINKS HE CAN!

If you think you are beaten, you are;
If you think you dare not, you don't
If you like to win but think you can't
It's almost a cinch you won't.

If you think you'll lose, you're lost,
For out in the world we find
Success begins with a fellow's will
It's all in the state of mind.

If you think you are out-classed, you are
You've got to think high to rise;
You've got to be sure of yourself before
You can ever win a prize.

Life's battles don't always go
To the stronger or faster man
But sooner or later the man who wins
Is the man who thinks he can.

Author Unknown

ABOVE
ALL
ELSE...

GET ME OUT OF THE WAY!

I pray and I plan and I properly perform
Hoping the Spirit might come.
Yet day after day life goes on the same way
And the hearts of the people grow numb.

Proud and pompous and elegant I stand
Thinking I know what to say.
Yet the Master is hidden all over the land
For I won't get out of the way.

My prayer dear God as I breathe a new breath
As humbly I seek divine grace,
To flood o'er my soul - encase every word
That all praise might fall on your face.

Stephen P. Dietzel

MY YOKE IS EASY
MY BURDEN LIGHT

Matthew 11:25-31

I had walked through life with a heavy load;
The journey was long, there were curves in the road.
I was all but defeated, my life had no zest,
Until God reached down and gave me His rest.
His yoke is easy, His burden is light;
He gives me new day where once there was night,
He is the leader, He carries the load;
Life is exciting as we walk down the road.
In the day by day journey He walks by my side,
He is my strength, He is my guide.

We laugh and we sing as we walk down the road;
Though the trials be many - He carries the load!
At times I fall, sometimes I fail, but He knows in the journey I can't quit,
For once in the yolk with Almighty God, No other yoke will fit.
He's chosen me and eternally matched my task with my given gifts;
He takes the burdens that come to me, and daily the load He lifts.
What a joy to realize no job is too big or too small.
The outcome is always in His hands - He lifts me from each fall.
The load is behind me, the stress is His, as we press on down the road.
Through struggles & pressures & trouble-filled times,
  I REST, for He carries the load!

Stephen P. Dietzel

Stephen P. Dietzel

I Knelt to Pray

I knelt to pray but not for long, I had too much to do.
I had to hurry and get to work for bills would soon be due.
So I knelt and said a hurried prayer, and jumped up off my knees.
My Christian duty was now done my soul could rest at ease . . .

All day long I had not time to spread a word of cheer;
No time to speak of Christ to friends, they'd laugh at me I'd fear.
No time, no time, too much to do, that was my constant cry,
No time to give to souls in need, but at last the time, the time to die.

I went before the Lord, I came, I stood with downcast eyes.
For in His hands God held a book: It was the book of life.
God looked into His book and said, "Your name I cannot find;
I once was going to write it down, but never found the time."

Winning is not a sometime thing, you don't win once-in-awhile, you don't do things right once-in-awhile, you do them right all the time.

(Vince Lombardi)

In man's finest hour, his greatest fulfillment to all he holds dear, is the moment when he has worked his heart out in a good cause and lies exhausted on the field of battle victorious.

(Vince Lombardi)

The quality of any man's life has got to be a full measure of that man's personal commitment to excellence and to victory regardless of what field he be in.

(Vince Lombardi)

A careful man I want to be - a little fellow follows me. I dare not go astray - for fear he'll go the self-same way.

(John Wooden)

On the fields of friendly strife are sown the seeds that on other fields and other days will reap the fruits of victory.

(Douglas MacArthur)

This is the lesson: Never give in...Never, Never, Never, Never...in nothing, great or small, large or petty - never give in except to convictions of honor or good taste.

(Winston Churchill)

Happy are those who dream dreams and are ready to pay the price to make them come true.

(L.J. Cardinal Suenens)

Great people are just ordinary people with an extraordinary amount of determination.

(Robert H. Schuller)

Stephen P. Dietzel

There's nobody else in the whole human race, with your kind of style and your kind of grace. There's nobody else exactly like you, there's nobody else like you.

(Author Unknown)

Why should we be in such desperate hast to succeed and in such desperate enterprises? If a man does not keep pace with his companions, perhaps it is because he hears the beat of a different drummer.

(Henry David Thoreau)

Nothing would be done at all if a man waited 'till he could do it so well that no one could find fault with it.

(Cardinal Newman)

Men can alter their lives if they can alter the attitudes of their mind.

(William James Bryant)

A successful person is one who went ahead and did the thing the rest of us never quite got around to doing.

(Author Unknown)

The most successful leaders are those who recognize the creative potential of everyone on their team and make productive use of it.

(Paul J. Meyer)

I'd rather do something that is great and fail than do nothing and succeed!
The greatest discovery of my generation is that human beings can alter their lives by altering their attitudes of mind.

(William James)

It is too much to ask people to be good, the best we can expect is to ask that people practice good habits.

(Aristotle)

72

Failure does not come in falling, but in failing to rise again. The man who removes mountains begins by carrying away small stones.

You can do a lot with a little that is totally dedicated.

(Robert H. Schuller)

The greatest accomplishments of man have resulted from the transmission of ideas with enthusiasm.

(Thomas Watson)

The smallest good deed is better than the grandest intention.

You see things as they are and you ask "Why?" I dream things that never were and ask "Why not?"

(George Bernard Shaw)

Hold fast to dreams, for if dreams die, life is a broken-winged bird that cannot fly.

(Langston Hughes)

Success is focusing the full power of all you are on what you have a burning desire to achieve.

(Wilferd Peterson)

Slow me down, Lord, and inspire me to send my roots deep into the soil of life's enduring values that I may grow toward the stars of my greater destiny.

My business is not to remake myself, but, to make the absolute best of what God made.

(Robert Browning)

To be what we are, and to become what we are capable of becoming is the only end of life.

(Robert Louis Stevenson)

Not having a goal is more to be feared than not reaching a goal. When you catch up with your goals, you are in trouble. The "is" must never catch up with the "ought."

(Robert H. Schuller)

Change your thoughts and you can change your world.

What you do with your problem is far more important that what your problem does to you.

To accomplish all that's possible, you have to attempt the impossible.

To be as much as I can be, I must dream of being more!

Thorough preparation makes its own luck.

(Joe Poyer)

Great spirit, help me never to judge another until I have walked in his moccasins for two weeks.

(Sioux Indian Prayer)

Our rewards in life will always be in direct proportion to our contribution.
You can achieve whatever you want in life when you help enough other people achieve what they want.

(Napoleon Hill)

There's a natural law that says you never get something without giving up something.

No man need live a minute longer as he is, because the Creator endowed him with the ability to change himself.

(J.C. Penney)

There is no security on this earth. There is only opportunity.

(Douglas MacArthur)

The speed of the leader determines the rate of the pack.

(Wayne Lukas)

It's not so much where you are, but the direction you're heading that counts.

None of the secrets of success will work unless you do.

(Fortune Cookie!)

You're never a loser until you quit trying.

(Mike Ditka)

Many receive advice, only the wise profit by it.

(Fortune Cookie!)

Sometimes the poorest man leaves his children the richest inheritance.

(Ruth E. Renkel)

Most people confuse wishing and wanting with pursuing. Place your trust in action. Act Now!

I'd rather be a failure at something I enjoy than be a success at something I hate.

(George Burns)

It takes as much courage to have tried and failed as it does to have tried and succeeded.

(Anne Morrow Lindbergh)

You'll never find a better sparring partner than adversity.

(Walt Schmidt)

Stephen P. Dietzel

There are no shortcuts to any place worth going.

(Beverly Sills)

"If you carry your childhood with you, you never become older."

(Abraham Sutzekever)

Happiness is found in doing, not merely possessing.

The elevator to success doesn't work. You'll have to take the stairs - one step at a time.

It is in doing that you become.

(Bob Richards)

No one is useless in this world who lightens the burden of it to anyone else . (Charles Dickens)

Everything comes if a man will only wait! A human being with a settled purpose must accomplish it; and nothing can resist a will that stakes even existence on its fulfillment!

(Disraeli)

No more effort is required to aim high in life, to demand abundance and prosperity, than is required to accept misery and poverty.

(Napoleon Hill)

One never knows what he might accomplish until he tries. Give things a chance to happen! Give success a chance to happen! It is impossible to win the race unless you venture to run, impossible to win the victory unless you dare to battle.

(Rich DeVos)

All who have accumulated great fortunes, first did a certain amount of dreaming, hoping, wishing, desiring and planning before they acquired money.

(Napoleon Hill)

Never ask men for more than they can give, but ask for all they can give.

(Gandhi)

A man's reach must exceed his grasp, else what's a heaven for?

(Robert Browning)

Every adversity carries with it the seed of an equal or greater benefit.

(W. Clement Stone)

Lonely people build walls instead of bridges.
Live in 'day-tight' compartments. Our business is not to see what lies dimly in the distance, but, to do what lies clearly at hand. Think of your life as an hourglass - only one grain of sand at once!

(Dale Carnegie)

Forget your own unhappiness - try to create a little happiness for others. When you are good to others, you are best to yourself.

(Dale Carnegie)

To prevent worry and fatigue, put enthusiasm into your work! Remember, no one was ever killed by lack of sleep. Worrying about insomnia does the damage...not the insomnia!

(Dale Carnegie)

Success is taking the hand you were dealt and making the best of it.

What you get by reaching your destination isn't nearly as important as what you become by reaching your destination.

The mass of men lead lives of quiet desperation and go to the grave with the song still in them. Things do not change; we change. To awaken is to be alive.

(Henry David Thoreau)

Stephen P. Dietzel

Nothing happens unless first a dream.

(Carl Sandburg)

Desire is the ingredient that makes the difference between the average performer and a champion.

The way you think is what causes your problems...you have to straighten out the way you think.

(Author Unknown)

Smiling is a good habit. We don't smile because we're happy, but, we're happy because we smile.

A successful person is one who is excited about his future before he gets there!

There is nothing either good or bad, but thinking makes it so.

(William Shakespeare)

Fight one more round - remembering that the man who always fights one more round is never whipped.

(James J. Corbett)

A person cannot travel within and stand still without.

(James Allen)

What lies behind us and what lies before us are tiny matters compared to what lies within us.

(Oliver Wendell Holmes)

The difference between an obstacle and an opportunity is our attitude toward it. Every opportunity has a difficulty and every difficulty has an opportunity.

(J. Sidlow Baxter)

The last of the human freedoms is to choose one's attitude in any given set of circumstances.

(Victor Frankel)

The ancestor of every action is a thought.

(Ralph Waldo Emerson)

We are not called to be successful, we are called to be faithful.

If at first you don't succeed, try reading the directions.

If you tell the truth, you don't have to remember anything.

(Mark Twain)

Nothing has any power over me other than that which I give it through my conscious thoughts.

(Anthony Robbins)

I know of no more encouraging fact than the unquestionable ability of man to elevate his life by conscious endeavor.

(Henry David Thoreau)

It is the greatest of all mistakes to do little because you can only do a little. Do what you can.

(Sydney Smith)

The air-currents of life jolt us out of line and try to keep us from achieving our goals. Unexpected weather can change our direction and strategy. We must adjust our thinking continually so we can live right.

(John Maxwell)

God prepares great men for great tasks by great trials.

(J. K. Gressett)

If you don't know where you are going, you will probably end up somewhere else.

(Laurence J. Peter)

Beware of posing as a "profound person" - Jesus became a baby!

(Oswald Chambers)

If I had life to live over again, I would spend less time preaching and speaking and more time studying the Bible and praying.

(Billy Graham)

You have to build a good character, you can't inherit it.

Nothing splendid has ever been achieved except by those who dared believe that something inside of them was superior to circumstance.

(Bruce Baron)

If we all did the things we are capable of doing, we would literally astound ourselves.

(Thomas A. Edison)

It is the mind that maketh good or ill, that maketh wretch or happy, rich or poor.

(Edmund Spenser)

Habit is either the best of servants or the worst of masters.

(Nathaniel Emmous)

Words are the thread on which we string our experience.

(Aldous Huxley)

What happens all around you is usually outside your control. The way you react to what's outside is inside your control.

There can be no transforming of darkness into light and of apathy into movement without emotion.

(Carl Jung)

Your circumstances may be uncongenial, but they shall not long remain so if you perceive an ideal and strive to reach it.

(James Allen)

Man's mind stretched to a new idea never goes back to its original dimensions.

(Oliver Wendell Holmes)

Go put your creed into your deed.

(Ralph Waldo Emerson)

Someday after we have mastered the winds, the waves, the tide and gravity, we shall harness for God the energies of love. Then, for the second time in the history of the world, man will have discovered fire.

(Teilhard de Chardin)

If you think your thought is powerful, your thought IS powerful.

(Thomas Toward)

The joy is in the journey, not the arrival at the destination.

Give a man a fish and he'll eat for a day; teach a man to fish and he'll eat for a lifetime.

You become what you consciously think about.

(Earl Nightingale)

A professional is one who can do his best work when he doesn't feel like it.

(Alistaire Cooke)

You may not know what the future holds, but you can know who holds your future.

The mind is like a TV set - when it goes blank, it's a good idea to turn off the sound.

(Communication Briefings)

The successful job is a portrait of the person who did it.

Revenge may get you even with the enemy, but forgetting the past may beat the enemy.

One percent doubt and you're out!

(Mark Victor Hansen)

The hardest thing in life to learn is which bridge to cross and which to burn.

(David Russell)

The very essence of leadership is that you have to have vision. You can't blow an uncertain trumpet.

(Theodore Hesburgh)

As a man thinks, so is he. As he continues to think, so he remains. Man thus, in a measure becomes a servant of his thoughts, and through his thoughts, he works out his affairs.

(Bobby Charleton)

If God says, "Move ahead," He will lead the charge and equip the move.

If you don't have a dream, and if I don't have a dream, how are we going to make a dream come true.

(Mary Martin)

You will become as small as your controlling desires, as great as your dominant aspiration.

(James Allen)

True wisdom is possessed by the man who closes his own mouth before someone else wants to.

Whatever the mind can conceive and believe, it can achieve.

(Napoleon Hill)

Man may fail over and over, but he is not a true failure until he blames another.

We are paid not for what we know, but for what we do with what we know.

(Peter Webster)

There is no right way to do a wrong thing.

A single conversation with a wise person, is worth a month's study of books.

(Old Chinese Proverb)

Success has a simple formula: Do your best, and people may like you.

(Sam Ewing)

Man is not the sum of what he has but the totality of what he does not yet have, of what he might have.

(John Paul Sartre)

Faith is the ability to...see the invisible...believe the incredible...to get the impossible.

(Paul and Dan Monaghan)

Stephen P. Dietzel

Make no little plans, they have no magic to stir man's blood and probably will not be realized. Make big plans, aim high in hope and in work, remembering that a noble and logical diagram will not die.

(Daniel H. Burnham)

No one can make you feel inferior without your consent.
If you imagine it, you can achieve it; if you can dream it, you can become it.

(William Arthur Ward)

God gave the "Ten Commandments" with more implied than "suggestions."

If you only look at what it is, you might never attain what it could be.

(Unknown)

Motivation is what gets you started. Habit is what keeps you going.

(Jim Ryun)

The problem is not the problem. The problem is my attitude about the problem.

If at first you don't succeed, you're running about average.

God always gives the best to those who leave the choice to Him.

Sleep no more!

(William Shakespeare)

Renew a right spirit within me.

(Psalm 51:10)

I have done my best in the race. I have run the full distance, I have kept the faith.

(Apostle Paul - II Timothy 4:7)

All things which are impossible with men are possible with God.

(Luke 18:27)

Peace I leave with you, My peace I give unto you: not as the world giveth, give I unto you. Let not your heart be troubled, neither let it be afraid.

(John 14:27

THE SEA OF GALILEE and the Dead Sea are made of the same water. It flows down, clear and cool, from the Hermon and the roots of the cedars of Lebanon. The Sea of Galilee makes beauty of it, for the Sea of Galilee has an outlet. It gets to give. It gathers in its riches that it may pour them out again to fertilize the Jordan plain. But the Dead Sea has no outlet. It gets to keep. That is the radical difference between selfish and unselfish men. We all do want life's enriching blessings; we ought to; they are divine benedictions. But some men get to give, and they are like Galilee; while some men get to keep and they are like the brackish water that covers Sodom and Gomorrah.

Author Unknown

If you have faith as a grain of mustard seed, you can say to this mountain move, and nothing shall be impossible.

(Matthew 17:20)

Come unto Me, all ye that labor and are heavy laden, and I will give you rest.
(Matthew 11:28)

If God be for us, who can be against us?

(Romans 8:31)

What things you desire, when you pray, believe that you receive them, and you shall have them.

(Mark 1:24)

Trust in the Lord with all your heart, and do not lean on your own understanding. In all your ways acknowledge Him and He will make your paths straight.

(Proverbs 3:5,6)

I am come that they might have life, and that they might have it more abundantly.

(John 10:10)

Confess your faults one to another, and pray one for another, that ye may be healed. The effectual prayer of a righteous man avails much.

(James 5:16)

God is our refuge and strength, a very present help in trouble.

(Psalm 46:1)

All things are possible to him who believes.

(Mark 9:23)

Ask, and it shall be given you; seek, and ye shall find; knock, and it shall be opened unto you.

(Matthew 7:7)

For God hath not given us the spirit of fear; but of power, and of love, and of a sound mind.

(II Timothy 1:7)

I have learned, in whatsoever state I am, therewith to be content.

(Philippians 4:11)

"Have I not commanded you? Be strong and courageous! Do not tremble or be dismayed, for the LORD your God is with you wherever you go."

(Joshua 1:9)

Be transformed by the renewing of your mind.

(Romans 12:2)

If any man is in Christ, he is a new creature: old things are passed away; behold all things are become new.

II Corinthians 5:17)

Cast thy burden upon the Lord, and He shall sustain thee: He shall never suffer the righteous to be moved.

(Psalm 55:22)

This one thing I do, forgetting those things that are behind, and reaching forth unto those things which are before, I press toward the mark for the prize of the high calling of God in Christ Jesus.

(Philippians 3:13-14)

I can do all things through Christ who strengths me.

(Philippians 4:13)

The kingdom of God is within you.

(Luke 7:21)

And you shall know the truth, and the truth shall make you free. If the Son therefore shall make you free, you shall be free indeed.

(John 8:32, 36)

Things which eye has not seen, and ear has not heard, and which have not entered into the heart of man, All that God has prepared for those that love Him.

(I Corinthians 2:9)

If you abide in me, and my words abide in you, you shall ask what you will and it shall be done unto you.

(John 15:7)

Stephen P. Dietzel

And whatsoever you shall ask in my name, that will I do, that the Father may be glorified in the Son.

(John 14:13)

I beseech you therefore, brethren, by the mercies of God, that you present your bodies a living sacrifice, holy, acceptable unto God, which is your reasonable service. And be not conformed to this world; but be transformed by the renewing of your mind, that you may prove what is that good, and acceptable, and perfect, will of God.

(Romans 12:1,2)

Those who wait upon the Lord shall renew their strength; they shall mount up with wings like eagles, they shall run and not be weary, they shall walk and not faint.

(Isaiah 40:31)

For I am persuaded, that neither death, nor life, nor angels, nor principalities, nor power, nor things present, nor things to come, nor height, nor depth, nor any other creature, shall be able to separate us from the love of God, which is in Christ Jesus our Lord.

(Romans 8:38, 39)

Be careful for nothing; but in every thing by prayer and supplication with thanksgiving let your requests be made known unto God. And the peace of God that passes all understanding, shall keep your hearts and minds through Christ Jesus.

(Philippians 4:6,7)

It's Me - Just Checking In

A minister passing through his church in the middle of the day,
Decided to pause by the altar and see who had come to pray.
Just then the back door opened, a man came down the aisle,
The minister frowned as he saw the man hadn't shaved in a while.

His shirt was kinda shabby and his coat was worn and frayed,
The man knelt, he bowed his head, then rose and walked away.
In the days that followed, each noon time came this chap,
Each time he knelt just for a moment, a lunch pail in his lap.

Well, the minister's suspicions grew, with robbery a main fear,
He decided to stop the man and ask him, "What are you doing here?"
The old man said, he worked down the road. Lunch was half an hour
Lunchtime was his prayer time, for finding strength and power.
"I stay only moments, see, because the factory is so far away;
As I kneel here talking to the Lord, this is kinda what I say:
"I JUST CAME AGAIN TO TELL YOU, LORD, HOW HAPPY I'VE BEEN,
SINCE WE FOUND EACH OTHER'S FRIENDSHIP AND YOU TOOK AWAY MY SIN.
DON'T KNOW MUCH OF HOW TO PRAY, BUT I THINK ABOUT YOU EVERYDAY.
SO, JESUS, THIS IS JIM CHECKING IN TODAY."

The minister feeling foolish, told Jim, that was fine.
He told the man he was welcome to come and pray just anytime.

Time to go, Jim smiled, said "Thanks." He hurried to the door.
The minister knelt at the altar, he'd never done it before.

His cold heart melted, warmed with love, and met with Jesus there.
As the tears flowed, in his heart as he repeated old Jim's prayer:

Stephen P. Dietzel

"I JUST CAME AGAIN TO TELL YOU, LORD, HOW HAPPY I'VE BEEN,
SINCE WE FOUND EACH OTHER'S FRIENDSHIP AND YOU TOOK AWAY MY SIN.
I DON'T KNOW MUCH OF HOW TO PRAY, BUT I THINK ABOUT YOU EVERYDAY.
SO, JESUS, THIS IS ME CHECKING IN TODAY."

Past noon one day, the minister noticed that old Jim hadn't come.
As more days passed without Jim, he began to worry some.
At the factory, he asked about him, learning he was ill.
The hospital staff was worried, but he'd given them a thrill.

The week that Jim was with them, brought changes in the ward.
His smiles, a joy contagious. Changed people, were his reward.
The head nurse couldn't understand why Jim was so glad,
When no flowers, calls or cards came, not a visitor he had.

The minister stayed by his bed, he voiced the nurse's concern:
No friends came to show they cared. He had nowhere to turn.

Looking surprised, old Jim spokeup and with a winsome smile;
"The nurse is wrong, she couldn't know, that in here all the while;
Everyday at noon,He's here, a dear friend of mine, you see,
He sits right down, takes my hand, leans over and says to me:

"I JUST CAME AGAIN TO TELL YOU, JIM, HOW HAPPY I HAVE BEEN,
SINCE WE FOUND THIS FRIENDSHIP, AND I TOOK AWAY YOUR SIN.
ALWAYS LOVE TO HEAR YOU PRAY, I THINK ABOUT YOU EACH DAY,
AND SO JIM, THIS IS JESUS CHECKING IN TODAY"

Many people will walk in and out of your life, but only true friends will leave footprints in your heart. May God hold you in the palm of His hand and Angels watch over you. But for those of us who are already His, He not only holds us in the palm of His hand, but has engraved our names there, and we are continually in His sight (Isaiah 49:16) Yes, I do love God. He is my source of existence and Savior He keeps me functioning each and everyday. Without Him, I will be nothing. Without him, I am nothing but with Him "I can do all things through Christ who strengthens me." [Philippians 4:13]

"WHATEVER IS TRUE whatever is noble, whatever is right, whatever is pure, whatever is lovely, whatever is admirable - if anything is excellent or praiseworthy - think about these things." (Philippians 4:9)

Be therefore followers of God as dear Children: and walk in love, as Christ also has loved us, and has given himself for us an offering and a sacrifice to God for a sweet-smelling savoir. Speaking to yourselves in psalms and hymns and spiritual songs, singing and making melody in your heart to the Lord. For we are members of His body, of His flesh and of His bones.

(Ephesians 5:1, 2, 19, 20)

My sheep hear my voice, and I know them, and they follow me; and I give unto them eternal life; and they shall never perish, neither shall any man pluck them out of my hand. My Father, who gave them to me, is greater than all; and no man is able to pluck them out of my Father's hand.

(John 10:27-29)

My people, who are called by My name will humble themselves, and pray and seek My face, and turn from their wicked ways, then I will hear from heaven, and I will hear from heaven, and I will forgive their sin and heal their land.

(II Chronicles 7:14)

I had many things to write, but I do not wish to write in pen and ink, but I hope to see you shortly and we shall speak face to face. Peace to you."

(III John 13-15)

About the Author:

Stephen Paul Dietzel was raised in the shadows of goal posts and stadium lights from the Louisiana bayou and the LSU Fighting Tigers to the mighty Hudson River and the West Point cadets, to the historic lowlands and the Fighting Gamecocks of South Carolina. Growing up the son of a nationally known football coach, he did not have to travel far to bask in the presence of some of America's finest athletes.

Steve has had the opportunity to speak in hundreds of settings from churches and youth rallies to seminars for senior adults. The life of enthusiasm is not an option for Steve, but a way of life. So many people go through a daily routine of existence without purpose and without hope. Steve's sincere prayer and promise is that this short book will provide a lift and an encouragement to all who read it.

Steve and his wife Judy advise senior adults about safe and secure retirement plans as well as long-term care planning. Steve has degrees in Business, a Masters in Education, and a Masters in Theology. Judy has undergraduate and Masters degrees in Education. Their son Paul is an honor student majoring in Mass Communications at Louisiana State University. They are each active members of Istrouma Baptist Church in Baton Rouge, Louisiana.

Please visit the Dietzels on their web page: http://www.TheDietzelGroup.com

What Others Have Said About Steve Dietzel . . .

REV. CLIFF BARROWS, Billy Graham Association: "It has been my privilege to have known Steve Dietzel for many years, going back to his student days at Furman University. We thank God for his life and ministry. His enthusiasm and commitment to Christ is contagious, and I am confident that his ministry will be a great blessing to all who hear him. I am very happy to commend him to you."

DR. ROY J. FISH, Professor of Evangelism, Southwestern Baptist Theological Seminary, Ft. Worth, Texas: "Because of his unusual gifts and rich background of experience, Steve Dietzel will be a tremendous blessing to any group who hears him. He talks the language of all ages, youth and parents as well. The quality of his life and the vitality of his message will be used to make a lasting impact for our Lord.

REV. JIMMY ROBERTSON, former Pastor, Milldale Baptist Church and International Ministries, Zachary, Louisiana: "Steve Dietzel has a burning desire in his heart to be used of God in a supernatural way as he ministers to the lost as well as the saints. He is a gifted and anointed preacher and teacher. His ministry will be a blessing to any church family. Without any reservations I can recommend him to your church for a revival, conference or any other occasion."

DR. JERRY SUTTON, Pastor, Two Rivers Baptist Church, Nashville, Tennessee: "Steve Dietzel, a member of a former congregation is my friend and encourager. He is specially gifted in communicating the dynamics of the Christian life. Steve's enthusiasm is contagious and his love for the Lord and people is obvious. Having observed Steve closely I can say quite honestly that I have never known a more warm and genuinely caring man. He is a minister to people who hurt. I see Jesus in him. I recommend Steve highly."

DR. ED YOUNG, Pastor, Second Baptist Church, Houston, Texas: "It is my privilege to commend to you Steve Dietzel. I was fortunate to have this young man on my church staff during a former pastorate, and I am confident of both his gifted competence and his "sold-out" commitment to our Lord."

www.ingramcontent.com/pod-product-compliance
Lightning Source LLC
Chambersburg PA
CBHW031253280526
45784CB00004B/1833

* 9 7 8 1 4 3 4 3 0 1 2 4 6 *